6th Workshop on Recent Advances in RST and Related Formalisms (RST 2017)

Santiago de Compostela, Spain
4 September 2017

ISBN: 978-1-5108-5286-0

INLG 2017

Proceedings of the 6th Workshop on
Recent Advances in RST and Related Formalisms

RST 2017

September 4, 2017
Santiago de Compostela, Spain

Preface

Rhetorical Structure Theory explains text coherence through relations held between parts of text, both in macro and microstructure (Mann and Thompson, 1988). RST is both a theory of discourse and a useful tool in various applications. In Linguistics, and as a theory of discourse, RST is a framework for the analysis of texts. It accounts for text coherence by postulating relations among units of discourse, which join together in a recursive fashion. It has provided important insights into text coherence, clause combining and discourse organization in language, across multiple languages. In Computational Linguistics, RST has proven useful in applications such as sentiment analysis and machine translation. A detailed description, including multiple references, is available from the RST web site: `http://www.sfu.ca/rst/`.

The 2017 Workshop on "RST and Related Formalisms" follows a series of events organized biannually first in Brazil (2007, 2009, 2011, 2013) as part of Brazilian NLP conferences, and then in Spain in 2015, as part of the Spanish NLP conference (`https://sites.google.com/site/workshoprst2015/`). The workshops have brought together the international community of researchers working in RST.

The 2017 Workshop was envisioned as a broader event, drawing program committee members and participants not only from RST, but from the wider field of discourse parsing and coherence relations, in RST and in related theories and approximations (SDRT, PDTB, CCR). We received 11 submissions, and each one was reviewed by two members of the Program Committee, according to the following criteria: originality; adequate theoretical support and methodology; quality of the analysis; clarity of presentation and relevant references. Of the 11 submissions, 10 were accepted. We also expanded the program with a demo session.

We would like to thank the members of the Program Committee for their commitment to the workshop. We look forward to another instance of the workshop in the future, and to much more excellent RST-based research.

REFERENCE:

Mann, W.C. and Thompson, S.A. 1988. Rhetorical Structure Theory: Toward a functional theory of text organization. Text-Interdisciplinary Journal for the Study of Discourse, 8(3), p. 243-281.

September 30, 2017

Bilbo - Basque Country (Spain)

Maite Taboada

Iria da Cunha

Erick Galani Maziero

Paula Cardoso

Juliano Desiderato Antonio

Mikel Iruskieta

Co-Organizers of RST 2017

Table of Contents

Workshop Program

08:30 - 09:00   Registration

09:00   Opening: Juliano A. Desiderato

9h — 1st session.   Chair: Iria da Cunha

- **9:00**   *Deliberation as Genre: Mapping Argumentation through Relational Discourse Structure*
  Oier Imaz and Mikel Iruskieta

- **9:30**   *The Good, the Bad, and the Disagreement: Complex ground truth in rhetorical structure analysis*
  Debopam Das, Manfred Stede and Maite Taboada

- **10:00**   *A Distributional View of Discourse Encapsulation: Multifactorial Prediction of Coreference Density in RST*
  Amir Zeldes

- **10:30**   *Rhetorical relations markers in Russian RST Treebank*
  Svetlana Toldova, Dina Pisarevskaya, Margarita Ananyeva, Maria Kobozeva, Alexander Nasedkin, Sofia Nikiforova, Irina Pavlova and Alexey Shelepov

11:00 - 11:30   Coffee Break

11:30 - 13.30 — 2nd session.   Chair: Juliano D. Antonio

- **11:30**   *Applying the Rhetorical Structure Theory in Alzheimer patients' speech*
  Anayeli Paulino de Jesús and Gerardo Sierra

- **12:00**   *Using lexical level information in discourse structures for Basque sentiment analysis*
  Jon Alkorta, Koldo Gojenola, Mikel Iruskieta and Maite Taboada

- **12:30**   *Framework for the Analysis of Simplified Texts Taking Discourse into Account: the Basque Causal Relations as Case Study*
  Itziar Gonzalez-Dios, Arantza Diaz de Ilarraza and Mikel Iruskieta

- **13:00**   *Using Rhetorical Structure Theory for Detection of Fake Online Reviews*
  Olu Popoola

13:30 - 14:30   Lunch

14:30 - 16:00 — 3rd session.   Chair: Debopam Das

- **11:30**   *"Haters gonna hate": challenges for sentiment analysis of Facebook comments in Brazilian Portuguese*
  Juliano D. Antonio and Ana Cristina Leatte Santin

- **11:30**   *Discourse Segmentation for Building a RST Chinese Treebank*
  Shuyuan Cao, Nianwen Xue, Iria da Cunha, Mikel Iruskieta and Chuan Wang

15:30   **Open Meeting**

16:30   **Coffee-break**

17:00   **Demo session**

- **11:30**   *rstWeb tool: demo session*
  Amir Zeldes

- **11:30**   *ArText: demo session*
  Iria da Cunha

19:00   **Workshop closure**

Deliberation as Genre: Mapping Argumentation through Relational Discourse Structure

Oier Imaz
oier.imaz@ehu.eus
University of the Basque Country
Vrije Universiteit Brussel
(UPV/EHU - VUB)
PRAXIS Research Group
Elhuyar plaza 2.
20018 Donostia, Gipuzkoa

Mikel Iruskieta
mikel.iruskieta@ehu.eus
University of the Basque Country
(UPV/EHU)
IXA Group for NLP
Manuel Lardizabal pasealekua 1.
20018 Donostia, Gipuzkoa

Abstract

Deliberation is an increasingly used concept in Argumentation Theory and Linguistic Analysis. But only recently research combined empirical and conceptual tool-boxes from these disciplines for the study of deliberative discourse. The aim of this article is to present a discursive analysis of deliberation as a genre using the relational discourse structure of texts. In particular, we want to see whether different features of deliberation genre map onto relational discourse structures of texts.To do so, authors analyze, in the framework of Rhetorical Structure Theory (RST), the relational discourse structure of a Basque-Spanish bilingual corpus of argumentative micro-texts written by citizens participating in a series of deliberative mini-publics. Results suggest that genre affects the relational discourse structures of texts and that we could analyze this effect in RST. Finally, we present, to our knowledge, the first annotated corpus-based genre analysis of the relational discourse structure of argumentative micro-texts (available online) with RST.

1 Introduction

Deliberation is an increasingly used concept in Argumentation Theory (Fairclough and Fairclough, 2013; van Eemeren, 2013). Argumentation Theory analyses deliberation as a genre, meaning discourse that is goal oriented, unfolds through stages and belongs to a discourse community (Bhatia, 2004). But only recently researches (Collins and Nerlich, 2015; Murray et al., 2013) focused on the linguistic analysis of deliberation as a genre.

The aim of this article is to present a discourse analysis of deliberation as a genre through the rhetorical structure of texts. We want to see whether the relational discourse structure of texts is influenced by different variables linking text to context: i) cultural variables (language) shaping the linguistic context of text (micro-context), ii) institutional design-choices (group composition) that feature the particular setting in which deliberation occurs (meso-context) and iii) stages of deliberation (macro-context). For Deliberative Democratic Theory and Argumentation Theory these three variables are relevant and affect the capacity of deliberation to achieve its purpose.

To do so, authors analyze the relational discourse structure of a Basque-Spanish bilingual corpus of argumentative micro-texts written by citizens participating in a series of deliberative mini-publics, in the framework of Rhetorical Structure Theory (RST) (Mann and Thompson, 1988).

Results suggest that the relational discourse structure of texts can be affected by the stage of discussion and design-choices, but not by the language of the participants.

Finally, we present, to our knowledge, the first annotated corpus-based genre analysis of the relational discourse structure of argumentative micro-texts (available online[1]) with RST, in which discourse structures map onto deliberative dialogues. The time-cost of manual analysis in the RST framework limits the size of the corpus and the scope for application of this method. But advances have

---

[1] The corpus could be consulted at `http://ixa2.si.ehu.es/diskurtsoa/rstfilo/`

Proceedings of the 6th Workshop Recent Advances in RST and Related Formalisms, pages 1–10,
Santiago de Compostela, Spain, September 4 2017. ©2017 Association for Computational Linguistics

been made for automatic discourse parsing of texts in Basque and Spanish (more info in Related Work Section).

2 Theoretical Framework: Deliberation as an Argumentation Genre

Argumentation is broadly defined here as the process through which people seek to reach conclusions through reasons (Fischer, 2012). Deliberation, on the other hand, is defined as a particular form of argumentation procedurally regulated by an ideal model, so that conclusions are reached only by *the force of the better argument* (Steiner, 2012). Both concepts testify for long and fruitful theoretical traditions: Argumentation Theory and Deliberative Democracy. Nevertheless, only recently they converged on the idea that deliberation is an argumentation 'genre' (Van Eemeren, 2016; Walton et al., 2014; Fairclough and Fairclough, 2013).

From the perspective of discourse studies, the key concept linking language and discourse is 'genre' (Miller, 1984). Genre entails that texts are goal-oriented, involve stages and both influence linguistic choices. First, texts are goal-oriented because genre defines texts as communicative events geared to shared purposes in different discourse communities (Swales, 1990). Second, genre involves stages, because to accomplish shared purposes communicative events are structured in series of functional steps. Finally, Taboada (2004) suggests that genre is realized at the text level and it determines its structural organization.

In this paper, text analysis will follow basic guidelines from Taboada (2004, p. 29-36). According to her, genre analysis involves: i) finding a structural formula that will represent instances of a genre and ii) analyzing their linguistic characteristics[2].

To complete the first task, we follow conventions from Argumentation Theory and, to complete the second task, we follow conventions from Rhetorical Structure Theory.

2.1 Deliberation Genre in Argumentation Theory

Texts in the corpus are contributions written by citizens in a deliberative mini-public.

The institutional point or shared purpose of political deliberation is "preserving the democratic political culture by means of deliberation" (van Eemeren, 2013, p. 27). Indeed, organizers made this purpose explicit in *The Konpondu Initiative*. For example, the presentation leaflet underlines that it was motivated by the commitment of political representatives to build peace and contribute to political normalization. And it adds "the opinion of society, of people like you, is a fundamental contribution to that end".[3] Moreover, the invitation letter[4] established as rule 'mutual respect'; the central aspect of deliberation from the perspective of Argumentation Theory.

To accomplish this general purpose, the ideal template of deliberation defines seven different stages (McBurney et al., 2007, p.6).[5] Nevertheless, this template should be adapted to real circumstances (Fairclough, 2016; Van Eemeren, 2016). In our case, texts collected inform over the *Opening* stage, or the question posed by the moderator. An *Inform-Propose* stage where citizen inform over their goals and perspectives and suggest possible courses of action. Next, a *Consider* stage where citizens consider a proposal placed by the moderator. To conclude, a *Revise* stage where proposals are accepted or rejected.

Finally, to advance towards the shared purpose citizens participating in a deliberative event are expected to fulfill a 'deliberative minimum' (Fairclough, 2016). In short, the ideal model of deliberative argumentation requires minimally "weighing reasons in favor of a claim against reasons against it (reasons supporting the counter-claim), or balancing each argument against a counter-argument" (Fair-

---

[2]It is specified step by step as follows: i) Identification of segments or series of segments; ii) Definition of the social purpose; iii) Functional labeling of stages; iv) Specify obligatory and optional stages, v) Devise a structural formula; vi) Analyze the semantic and lexical-grammatical features for each stage (Taboada, 2004, p. 36)

[3]Promotional leaflet of the *Konpondu Initiative* released by the Basque Government and collected in the course of this research.

[4]Invitation letter sent by Juan Karlos Goinetxea major of Bermeo to citizens, collected in the course of this research.

[5]Deliberation dialogue begins with an open question (*Opening*), followed by discussion on goals, constraints and perspectives (*Inform*), next proposals are placed (*Propose*), jointly considered (*Consider*), accepted or rejected (*Revise*) and an option is recommend (*Recommend*) before deliberation dialogue is closed (*Conclude*).

clough and Fairclough, 2013, p. 50).

2.2 Argumentative Discourse in RST

Regarding the linguistic characteristics of deliberation genre, Taboada suggests that genre analysis should focus on variations as realized in the information structure (rhetorical relations), thematic structure (realization and progression) and cohesive structure (chains) of a text in its social and communicative context. Indeed, according to her, the relevant level of genre analysis is more textual than lexical-grammatical[6] (Taboada, 2004, p. 29-32). Our research focuses on one of those aspects in particular: the relational discourse structure. Coherence relations reflect the relational discourse structure of texts and could be analyzed with RST.

RST is an approach in which an analyst describes coherence between text fragments. To describe coherence, the analyst combines three main concepts: *a)* Elementary Discourse Units (EDU, henceforth) are independent or adverbial clauses. *b)* Recursive coherent relations between text fragments that have different effects on the reader: pragmatic or presentational relations and semantic or subject matter relations. As relations are recursive, a coherence relation can be a text fragment of other relation. *c)* Nuclearity, that is, the importance of a text fragment within the relation. Guided by the text, the analyst can describe which fragments are more important in the coherence relation (nucleus or satellite function) and also to other EDUs (central unit of a text).

Finally, we cluster coherence relations following Benamara and Taboada (2015) as Temporal, Thematic, Structural and Argumentative. The Argumentative Opposition subclass includes coherence relations that fulfill "the role of the classical thesis-antithesis structure." (Taboada and Gómez-González, 2012, p.35) Therefore, we take the argumentative opposition subclass to represent the 'deliberative minimum' in the relational discourse structures of texts in our corpus.

3 Methodology

The annotation of the corpus follows basic guidelines of RST implemented in the "Multilingual Discourse TreeBank" (Iruskieta et al., 2015a). We will classify texts in regards to coherence relation classes conforming their relational discourse structure (Benamara and Taboada, 2015). Finally, we will statistically analyze whether different contextual variables (relevant for the genre of deliberation) affect the relational discourse structure of texts in our corpus.

3.1 Corpus

Texts in the corpus are contributions made by citizens in a deliberative exercise named *The Konpondu Initiative*[7]. This initiative was held by the Basque Autonomous Government between 2007 and 2009 to foster citizens' participation in the resolution of the Basque conflict[8]. Texts are argumentative microtexts written by participants to assist their oral presentations. In short, they are fixed snapshots of different stages of the deliberative dialogue that took place in *The Konpondu Initiative*.

Mini-publics could be divided into two different phases depending on their structure. In the first phase, participants were called to express their opinion in response to a trigger question[9] placed by the moderator, at the beginning of the exercise. Besides, participants were invited to reflect on the most interesting contributions made by others. In the second phase, the first question[10] was more precise; it asked participants to underline different aspects (risks/opportunities/doubts). And, in addition to the concluding round, a direct question[11] on the *Consultation Law* (Keating and Bray, 2006) was introduced in the middle of the exercise.

The complete set is composed of 2,850 plain texts ordered by language, group composition, stage of

---

[7]We want to thank Gorka Espiau and the *Agirre Lehendakaria Center*, Aitziber Blanco and Paul Rios from *Lokarri*, Jorge de la Herran from *Agora* and Igor Ahedo and Asier Blas from *Parte-Hartuz* (EHU) for helping us recollecting the documentation of *The Konpondu Initiative*.

[8]The initiative provided support for citizens participation via citizen fora held in 101 municipalities (162 fora), the diaspora (28 fora), the University (6 fora) and the youth council (6 fora), as well as a web fora (konpondu.net) where more than 20,000 comments were collected and over 1,000,000 hits documented

[9]In the current situation, what initiatives could contribute to a new opportunity for peace?

[10]In nowadays situation what problems and opportunities do you see to reach peace and political normalization?

[11]Do you agree that citizens be consulted to unlock the current situation?

---

[6]On the contrary, lexical-grammatical features of texts and the realization of the three meta-functions in language are more closely related to register than they are to genre.

Language	Texts	Relations	Words
Basque	100	1319	8900
Spanish	100	1205	11166
Total	**200**	**2524**	**20066**

Table 1: Corpus statistics

discussion, date, and town. As we show in Table 1, the corpus we present here is a selection of 200 texts using length as a general criterion, to capture those with denser discourse relational structures. We built a comparable set for both languages considering different stages of discussion and group-compositions.

3.2 Annotation, Evaluation and Classification

We annotated this Argumentative Basque-Spanish Treebank following the standard methodology in RST. We evaluated the reliability of the corpus following a two step process, first, implementing a qualitative evaluation method (Iruskieta et al., 2015a) and, second, by comparing RS-trees annotated by each annotator using the on-line freely available tool RSTeval (Maziero et al., 2009).[12]

Firstly, a novel annotator (A1) annotated some texts in both languages with the RSTTool (O'Donnell, 2000), following the standard way to annotate in RST: segmenting the text and, then, building the RS-tree modularly and incrementally (Pardo, 2005).

Secondly, a RST analyst (A2) annotated 20 texts (10 in Spanish and 10 in Basque) following the same methodology.

Thirdly, we compared RS-trees of A1 and A2 following a qualitative evaluation method proposed by (Iruskieta et al., 2015a) in two ways: a) with the extended set of RST relations and b) comparing a collapsed set of RST relations.

Fourthly, both annotators agreed on ideal templates or macro-structures on a case by cases basis. The annotation of the corpus was recomposed and, based on harmonized RS-trees, the annotation of relations was validated using RSTeval.

Fifthly, all the annotation data was automatically enriched morphosyntactically (lemmatized and POS-tagged) with Eustagger (Aduriz et al., 2003) for Basque and FreeLing (Carreras et al., 2004)

for Spanish and it was exported to a database and showed in a friendly web-service environment using some tools developed in Iruskieta et al. (2015b).

Finally, coherence relations were clustered in classes following Benamara and Taboada (2015) and texts classified by their relational discourse structure and formatted for statistical analysis.

3.2.1 Discourse Segmentation and Central Unit annotation

Example (1) is a text selected from our Basque corpus (translations are ours), to explain the segmentation and central unit detection tasks. We segmented the text manually into Elementary Discourse Units (EDUs) following Iruskieta et al. (2015b). EDUs are independent sentences and adverbial clauses. The decision to segment manually was taken because texts were written by citizens; meaning they are full of grammatical mistakes (and a lot verbal ellipsis) and automatic segmentation will loose some EDUs (and therefore relations in subsequent phases) and produce more errors.

(1) [Espainiako alderdi nagusiek ez dute nahi ikusi geu geure artean ondo konpontzea.]₁ [Elkarrizketa edukitzerakoan,]₂ **[norberaren "pretentsioak" apur bat bajatu behar dira,]₃** [akordio txikiak lortzeko,]₄ [eta gero akordio handietara heltzeko.]₅ [Ondo dago herritarren artean foroak eta hitz egitea,]₆ [baina politikoek (euskaldunak barne) ahalegin guztiak egiten dute,]₇ elkarrizketa erreal bat edukitzeko?]₈ [13] [FIL965-2-83-EUS][14]

After segmentation, we have annotated the main topic of the text or the most important idea of the citizen. This EDU will be the central unit of the RS-tree in the following annotation task[15]. In this

---

[13][Main Spanish political parties don't want to see us make do well among ourselves.]₁ [When having dialogue,]₂ **[each should lower her "ambitions",]₃** [to reach small agreements]₄ [and, then, arrive at major ones.]₅ [It is ok that citizens to talk to each other and fora,]₆ [but politicians (including Basques) do everything they can]₇ [to have a real dialogue?]₈

[14]Text ID-Question-Group-Language.

[15]The Central Unit is considered the correlate in RST to the Central Claim of an argumentation scheme (Peldszus and Stede, 2016) and important for future steps in the annotation of this corpus.

---

[12]RSTeval can be tested at http://www.nilc.icmc.usp.br/rsteval/.

text, we think that the most important sentence of the three is composed of segments 2 to 5 and if we put off all the adverbial clauses of this example, the main EDU is in bold type (EDU_3).

3.2.2 Annotation and Evaluation of Rhetorical Relations

After determining the main topic of the text, as seen in the Example 2, one annotator has labeled the entire corpus, and a part of the corpus was double annotated (A1 and A2) to measure the inter-annotator agreement.

> (2) ANTITHESIS (s ("1"), n (INTERPRETA-
> TION (n (CIRCUMSTANCE (s ("2"), n
> (PURPOSE (n ("**3**"), s (SEQUENCE (n
> ("4"), n ("5"))))))), s (CONCESSION (s
> ("6"), n (PURPOSE (n ("7"), s ("8"))))))))))
> [FIL965-2-83-EUS]

We evaluated the most difficult task of the rhetorical annotation, which is the relation labeling in regards to RST extended and collapsed relation-sets. Results of the qualitative evaluation revealed low (30%) and moderate (46%) inter-coder agreement subsequently for extended and collapsed relation-sets. The comparative analysis showed differences regarding central unit and nuclearity explaining, partially, low agreement. In short, the interpretation was not very different, but annotators formalized trees in different ways.

We tried that to reduce the ambivalence of interpretations harmonizing the macro-structures of RS-trees at each stage, and we realized we had to change some decisions taken to build the corpus. Initially, we analyzed texts responding to different aspects of the same question as independent text-units[16]. For example, we differentiated as independent text-units texts underlining 'problems' and 'opportunities' in response to the same question. But taken together we found most texts at this stage were structured with a central claim and a satellite of a SOLUTION-HOOD relation. This approach diminished the ambivalence of interpretation between annotators in regards to central unit detection and, correspondingly,

TextID	Matches	Recall	Precision
FIL102	43 of 49	0.934	0.877
FIL196	50 of 51	0.980	0.980
FIL1264	29 of 35	0.828	0.828
FIL1713	56 of 61	0.918	0.918
FIL2480	36 of 43	0.947	0.837
FIL2517	31 of 41	0.756	0.756

Table 2: Inter-annotator agreement of relation assignment using RSTeval, after a training session and harmonizing segmentation and scope of the rhetorical relations

affected positively regarding the agreement in relation labeling.

After a training session for the novel annotator, we recomposed the corpus following new guidelines and re-annotated it.

Finally, taking harmonized RS-trees based on macro-structural templates as a departure point for the annotation of texts at each stage of discussion, we re-annotated a sample of the original corpus and measured inter-coder agreement using the freely available on-line tool RSTeval (Table 2).

3.2.3 Text Classification, Cluster relations and Statistical Analysis

At the end, we were able to classify each text according to i) stage (1st and 2nd phase and initial (*Inform/Propose*), middle (*Consider*) or final stage (*Revise*)), ii) language (Basque or Spanish) and iii) group composition (linguistically heterogeneous or homogeneous)[17].

To answer our research questions, we classify coherence relations[18] in classes according to the taxonomy presented by Benamara and Taboada (2015) as follows: a) Temporal class[19]. b) Structuring class[20]. c) Thematic class is further divided in two sub-

---

[16]The reason to take that decision was that in the original reports those aspects of citizens' responses were written separately.

[17]i) and ii) are relevant aspects of deliberation genre from the perspective of Linguistic Analysis and Argumentation Theory. ii) and iii) are relevant aspects of deliberation genre from the perspective of Deliberative Democratic Theory (Caluwaerts and Deschouwer, 2014).

[18]This taxonomy also includes more semantically oriented relations as, for example, topic-comment SDRT relations. In this case, we have used it to classify only relations annotated in our corpus.

[19]Only includes SEQUENCE.

[20]CONJUNCTION, DISJUNCTION and LIST.

Class	Spanish Set						Basque Set					
	Heter.		Homog.		Total		Heter.		Homog.		Total	
Temporal	7	1.1%	4	0.7%	**11**		8	1.1%	5	0.9%	**13**	
Structuring	96	15.5%	95	16.2%	**191**		112	14.8%	97	18.0%	**209**	
Elaboration	116	18.7%	110	19.7%	**226**		157	20.7%	132	24.4%	**289**	
Framing	69	11.1%	81	14.5%	**150**		70	9.2%	41	7.6%	**111**	
Causal	105	16.9%	87	15.6%	**192**		126	16.6%	75	13.9%	**201**	
Purpose	55	8.9%	42	7.5%	**97**		55	7.2%	52	9.6%	**107**	
Support	105	16.9%	92	16.5%	**197**		158	20.8%	86	15.9%	**244**	
Opposition	68	11.0%	46	8.3%	**114**		73	9.6%	52	9.6%	**125**	

Table 3: Total relations per class by language and group composition.

classes: Elaboration[21] and Framing [22]. *d)* Argumentative class, divided in two subclasses: Causal [23] and Argumentative; and the latter further divided in two subclasses: Support [24] and Opposition [25][26].

Finally, to get the most informative approximation possible we cluster relations at the lower level of the hierarchy of each class and we order classes from less argumentative (Structuring) to more argumentative (Argumentative Opposition) in the light of the 'deliberative minimum'[27]. We test for high correlation among our independent variables excluding multicollinearity, and we make an ordinal logistic regression taking relation class as our dependent variable and stage, group-composition and language as our independent variables.

4 Results

In Table 3 we summarize the type and the frequency of each relation per subclass, group composition, and language. At first sight, we could see that, except for texts written in Basque in heterogeneous groups, each column follows the same order from most frequent to less frequent relation class (Argumentative, Thematic, Structuring, and Tempo-

---

[21] ELABORATION, SUMMARY, RESTATEMENT, MEANS and we have also included PREPARATION.

[22] BACKGROUND and CIRCUMSTANCE.

[23] CAUSE, RESULT, PURPOSE, CONDITIONAL group and we have also included SOLUTION-HOOD.

[24] MOTIVATION, EVIDENCE, JUSTIFY, EVALUATION, INTERPRETATION and we also included ENABLEMENT.

[25] CONTRAST, CONCESSION and ANTITHESIS.

[26] JOINT and UNION were excluded from clustering and, therefore, not considered for analysis and interpretation.

[27] We order them from less to more argumentative as follows: Structuring—Temporal—Elaboration—Framing—Causal—Purpose—Argumentative Support—Argumentative Opposition.

Phase	First Phase		Second Phase		
Class	Prop.	Rev.	Inf.	Cons.	Rev.
Non-arg.	**56%**	**60%**	**45%**	**40%**	**45%**
Arg.	44%	39%	**54%**	**59%**	**55%**

Table 4: Stages per phase and argumentative vs non-argumentative classes.

Source	W. Chi-Squ.	Df.	Sig.
G. Comp.	6.245	1	**0.012**
Stage	35.090	4	**0.000**
Language	0.181	1	0.670

Table 5: Tests of Model Effects

ral). Within classes, there are more Elaborative relations than Framing relations and more Argumentative than Causal.

In Table 4 we have dichotomized argumentative and non-argumentative classes per phase. Results show that, contrary to our expectations, the balance between argumentative and non-argumentative classes only differs slightly through stages within the same phase. But, it is interesting to see that there are differences if we compare both phases: in the first phase we find more non-argumentative class relations but, in the second phase, argumentative class relations score higher than in the first.

In response to our research questions, the Tests of Model Effects (Table 5) show that the stage of discussion and the composition of the group have a significant effect on the prediction of whether texts will be more argumentative. On the contrary, language has not a statistically significant effect.

To get a more detailed approximation of the directionality and size of these effects, we summarize main results of the ordinal logistic regression in Table 6.

Our first research question asks whether the lan-

Parameter	B.	Hypothesis Test				Exp(B)	95% Wald CI for Exp(B)	
		W. Chi-Sq.	Df.	Sig.			Lower	Upper
Heterog.	0.178	6.245	1	**0.012**	1.195	1.039	1.374
Homog.	0	.	.	.	1	.	.
Propose (I)	-0.449	14.154	1	**0.000**	0.639	0.505	0.807
Revise (I)	-0.590	17.142	1	**0.000**	0.555	0.420	0.733
Inform (II)	-0.216	3.253	1	0.071	0.806	0.638	1.019
Consider (II)	-0.026	0.047	1	0.828	0.974	0.771	1.232
Revise (II)	0	.	.	.	1	.	.
Spanish	-0.030	0.181	1	0.670	0.970	0.844	1.115
Basque	0	.	.	.	1	.	.

Table 6: Parameter Estimates

guage has an effect on the relational discourse structure of texts. Results show that the odds of texts written in Spanish being more argumentative are almost equal in comparison to those written in Basque. Therefore, language does not have a statistically significant effect on the degree of argumentativeness of texts in our corpus.

Our second research question asks whether the composition of the group has an effect on the relational discourse structure of texts. In this case, results show that the odds of texts being more argumentative are slightly higher (1.195; 95% CI, 1.039 to 1.374) in linguistically heterogeneous groups than in homogeneous groups. The difference is rather small, but the effect is statistically significant ($x^2(1)$=6.245, p=.012).

Finally, stages of discussion have an effect on the relational discourse structure of texts in our corpus, but this effect is statistically significant only of both stages in the first phase.

In the second phase, results show that the odds of the relational discourse structure of texts being more argumentative are similar at any stage of discussion. It is slightly lower at the *Inform* stage, but not significantly. On the contrary, at any stage in the first phase, the odds of the relational discourse structure of texts being more argumentative are lower in comparison to our reference category. This result is especially interesting because the question was the same at both phases, and we used the same macrostructural template.

In this case, the odds of texts in the *Revise* stage in the first phase being more argumentative are half (.555; 95% CI, .420 to .733) that of those in the same stage in the second phase, a statistically significant effect, $x^2(1)$=17.142, p<.001.

In sum, results show that the stage of discussion and the composition of the group have an effect on the relational discourse structure of texts in our corpus, but not the language. The odds ratios of being more argumentative are higher in the second phase and in linguistically heterogeneous groups. The size of this effect is greater for stages but rather small of group composition. These results may suggest the relational structures of these texts have common patterns associated with their genre. But further analysis is necessary, for example, including other variables or comparison to other genres.

5 Related Works

This research builds on previous attempts to analyze argumentation using RST.

Azar (1999) was first to propose RST as an alternative to the so-called "Toulmin Model" (Toulmin, 1958) for the analysis of argumentation. He used the satellite-nucleus distinction to identify arguments and conclusions for five types of relations: EVIDENCE, ANTITHESIS and CONCESSION (persuader), JUSTIFY (justifier), and MOTIVATION (incentive).

More recently, Green (2010; 2015), suggested the "Toulmin model" is more appropriate, but she outlined a proposal (ArgRST) where data and claim of an argument are represented respectively as the satellite and nucleus of an RS-tree.

Texts in our corpus are similar to the 'Postdam Corpus' (Peldszus and Stede, 2016; Stede et al., 2016) composed of 112 argumentative micro-texts written in response to trigger questions aimed at getting argumentatively dense texts. Authors conduct a parallel annotation using different methods for the analysis of discourse structures —Segmented Discourse Representation Theory (SDRT) and Rhetorical Structure Theory (RST)— and argumentation schemes (Freeman, 2011).

On the other hand, Hirst et al. (2014) combine linguistically enriched RST parsing based on HILDA discourse parser, and content analysis to analyze argumentation in political speech. They applied their model to the analysis of issue framing and ideological position in historical and contemporary proceedings of British, Canadian and Dutch parliaments.

These studies (Hirst et al., 2014; Stede et al., 2016) share that, despite limitations (Biran and Rambow, 2011), rhetorical structures can be considered appropriate for the analysis of the discourse structure of argumentative texts. But, they invite to the parallel annotation of argumentation schemes and relational discourse structures to enhance their translatability.

Regarding the analysis of argumentation in Basque and Spanish using RST, previous research shows that the nucleus of a rhetorical tree can be seen as the central claim of an argumentation scheme (Iruskieta et al., 2014). Moreover, promising advances have been made regarding automatic segmentation for Spanish[28] and Basque[29] (Iruskieta and Zapirain, 2015), central unit detection[30] (Bengoetxea et al., 2017) and causal coherence relation annotation in the baseline hierarchical level of the RS-tree (Kortajarena, 2016).

6   Conclusions and future work

First, in this paper, we report the creation of a Basque-Spanish bilingual corpus composed by 200 argumentative micro-texts. We have annotated the corpus following usual standards of RST and results are freely available for further analysis in an online database[31]. To our knowledge, this is the first genre

---

[28]The Spanish segmenter DiSeg can be tested online at http://sistema-artext.com/diseg/ (da Cunha et al., 2017).

[29]The segmenter can be tested online at http://ixa2.si.ehu.es/EusEduSeg/EusEduSeg.pl.

[30]The central unit (CU) detector can be tested online at http://ixa2.si.ehu.es/CU-detector/.

[31]The annotated corpus can be consulted online at http://ixa2.si.ehu.es/diskurtsoa/rstfilo/.

analysis of the relational discourse structure of texts applied to deliberative discourse.

Second, the analysis of relation classes has shown that the composition of the group and stages of discussion significantly affect the relational discourse structure of texts. Indeed, texts from groups with participants from different linguistic communities and more controversial questions ruling discussion are closer to the 'deliberative minimum.'

Finally, besides statistically significant differences and given the small size of effects, we could also suggest there are common patterns. Therefore, it is interesting for future research to see whether these patterns are unique and, therefore, genre related or common to other corpora from different genres.

Further steps will follow recommendations regarding parallel annotation of RS-trees and argumentation schemes (Stede et al., 2016). We will also linguistically enrich the annotation signaling Discourse Relational Devices following (2013).

Acknowledgments

This study was carried out within the framework of the following projects: IXA-CLARIN-K Centre, IXA group, Research Group (GIU16/16) and TUNER (TIN2015-65308-C5-1-R). Science and Society (IT644-13), PRAXIS Research Group.
We would like to thank Esther Miranda and Kike Fernandez (IXA Group) for their help in designing the web page.

References

[Aduriz et al.2003] Itziar Aduriz, Izaskun Aldezabal, Inaki Alegria, J Arriola, A Díaz de Ilarraza, Nerea Ezeiza, and Koldo Gojenola. 2003. Finite state applications for Basque. In *EACL 2003 Workshop on Finite-State Methods in Natural Language Processing*, pages 3–11.

[Azar1999] Moshe Azar. 1999. Argumentative text as rhetorical structure: An application of Rhetorical Structure Theory. *Argumentation*, 13(1):97–114.

[Benamara and Taboada2015] Farah Benamara and Maite Taboada. 2015. Mapping different rhetorical relation annotations: A proposal. In *Proceedings of the Fourth Joint Conference on Lexical and Computational Semantics, * SEM*, volume 2012, pages 147–152.

[Bengoetxea et al.2017] Kepa Bengoetxea, Aitziber Atutxa, and Mikel Iruskieta. 2017. Un detector de la unidad central de un texto basado en técnicas de aprendizaje automático en textos científicos para el euskera. *Procesamiento del Lenguaje Natural*, 58:37–44.

[Bhatia2004] Vijay Bhatia. 2004. *Worlds of written discourse: A genre-based view*. A&C Black.

[Biran and Rambow2011] Or Biran and Owen Rambow. 2011. Identifying justifications in written dialogs by classifying text as argumentative. *International Journal of Semantic Computing*, 5(04):363–381.

[Caluwaerts and Deschouwer2014] Didier Caluwaerts and Kris Deschouwer. 2014. Building bridges across political divides: Experiments on deliberative democracy in deeply divided Belgium. *European Political Science Review*, 6(03):427–450.

[Carreras et al.2004] Xavier Carreras, Isaac Chao, Lluis Padró, and Muntsa Padró. 2004. Freeling: An open-source suite of language analyzers. In *LREC*, pages 239–242.

[Collins and Nerlich2015] Luke Collins and Brigitte Nerlich. 2015. Examining user comments for deliberative democracy: A corpus-driven analysis of the climate change debate online. *Environmental Communication*, 9(2):189–207.

[da Cunha et al.2017] Iria da Cunha, M Amor Montané, and Luis Hysa. 2017. The artext prototype: An automatic system for writing specialized texts. *EACL 2017*, pages 57–60.

[Fairclough and Fairclough2013] Isabela Fairclough and Norman Fairclough. 2013. *Political discourse analysis: A method for advanced students*. Routledge.

[Fairclough2016] Isabela Fairclough. 2016. Deliberative discourse. *The Routledge Handbook of Critical Discourse Analysis. London: Routledge*.

[Fischer2012] Frank Fischer. 2012. *The argumentative turn revisited: public policy as communicative practice*. Duke University Press.

[Freeman2011] James B Freeman. 2011. *Argument Structure: Representation and Theory*. Springer Science & Business Media.

[Green2010] Nancy L. Green. 2010. Representation of argumentation in text with Rhetorical Structure Theory. *Argumentation*, 24(2):181–196.

[Green2015] Nancy L Green. 2015. Identifying argumentation schemes in genetics research articles. *NAACL HLT 2015*, pages 12–21.

[Hirst et al.2014] Graeme Hirst, Vanessa Wei Feng, Christopher Cochrane, and Nona Naderi. 2014. Argumentation, ideology, and issue framing in parliamentary discourse. In *ArgNLP*.

[Iruskieta and Zapirain2015] Mikel Iruskieta and Benat Zapirain. 2015. Euseduseg: A dependency-based EDU segmentation for Basque. *Procesamiento del Lenguaje Natural*, 55:41–48.

[Iruskieta et al.2014] Mikel Iruskieta, Arantza Díaz de Ilarraza, and Mikel Lersundi. 2014. The annotation of the central unit in rhetorical structure trees: A key step in annotating rhetorical relations. In *COLING*, pages 466–475.

[Iruskieta et al.2015a] Mikel Iruskieta, Iria Da Cunha, and Maite Taboada. 2015a. A qualitative comparison method for rhetorical structures: identifying different discourse structures in multilingual corpora. *Language resources and evaluation*, 49(2):263–309.

[Iruskieta et al.2015b] Mikel Iruskieta, Arantza Diaz de Ilarraza, and Mikel Lersundi. 2015b. Establishing criteria for RST-based discourse segmentation and annotation for texts in Basque. *Corpus Linguistics and Linguistic Theory*, 11(2):303–334.

[Keating and Bray2006] Michael Keating and Zoe Bray. 2006. Renegotiating sovereignty: Basque nationalism and the rise and fall of the ibarretxe plan. *Ethnopolitics*, 5(4):347–364.

[Kortajarena2016] Axier Kortajarena. 2016. Koherentziazko diskurtso erlazioen detekzio automatikoa patroien bidez: XMLko erlazio-egiturak oinarri hartuta. *HAP master work*.

[Mann and Thompson1988] William C. Mann and Sandra A. Thompson. 1988. Rhetorical structure theory: Toward a functional theory of text organization. *Text-Interdisciplinary Journal for the Study of Discourse*, 8(3):243–281.

[Maziero et al.2009] Erick Galani Maziero, Thiago Alexandre Salgueiro Pardo, and Núcleo Interinstitucional de Lingüística Computacional. 2009. Automatização de um método de avaliação de estruturas retóricas. In *Proceedings of the RST Brazilian Meeting*, pages 1–9.

[McBurney et al.2007] Peter McBurney, David Hitchcock, and Simon Parsons. 2007. The eightfold way of deliberation dialogue. *International Journal of Intelligent Systems*, 22(1):95–132.

[Miller1984] Carolyn R Miller. 1984. Genre as social action. *Quarterly Journal of speech*, 70(2):151–167.

[Murray et al.2013] Tom Murray, Xiaoxi Xu, and Beverly Park Woolf. 2013. An exploration of text analysis methods to identify social deliberative skill. In *International Conference on Artificial Intelligence in Education*, pages 811–814. Springer.

[O'Donnell2000] Michael O'Donnell. 2000. RSTTool 2.4: a markup tool for Rhetorical Structure Theory. In *Proceedings of the first international conference on Natural language generation-Volume 14*, pages 253–256. Association for Computational Linguistics.

[Pardo2005] Thiago Alexandre Salgueiro Pardo. 2005. *Métodos para análise discursiva automática*. Ph.D. thesis, Instituto de Ciências Matemáticas e de Computação.

[Peldszus and Stede2016] Andreas Peldszus and Manfred Stede. 2016. Rhetorical structure and argumentation structure in monologue text. In *Proceedings of the 3rd Workshop on Argument Mining*, pages 103–112. ACL.

[Stede et al.2016] Manfred Stede, Stergos Afantenos, Andreas Peldszus, Nicholas Asher, and Jeremy Perret. 2016. Parallel discourse annotations on a corpus of short texts. In *Proceedings of the International Conference on Language Resources and Evaluation (LREC), Portoroz*, pages 1051–1058.

[Steiner2012] Jürg Steiner. 2012. *The foundations of deliberative democracy: Empirical research and normative implications*. Cambridge University Press.

[Swales1990] John Swales. 1990. *Genre analysis: English in academic and research settings*. Cambridge University Press.

[Taboada and Das2013] Maite Taboada and Debopam Das. 2013. Annotation upon annotation: Adding signalling information to a corpus of discourse relations. *D&D*, 4(2):249–281.

[Taboada and Gómez-González2012] Maite Taboada and María de los Ángeles Gómez-González. 2012. Discourse markers and coherence relations: Comparison across markers, languages and modalities. *Linguistics and the Human Sciences*, 6(1-3):17–41.

[Taboada2004] Maite Taboada. 2004. *Building coherence and cohesion: Task-oriented dialogue in English and Spanish*, volume 129. John Benjamins Publishing.

[Toulmin1958] Stephen Toulmin. 1958. The uses of argument. *Cambridge, UK*.

[van Eemeren2013] Frans H van Eemeren. 2013. Strategic maneuvering in argumentative discourse in political deliberation. *Journal of Argumentation in Context*, 2(1):10–31.

[Van Eemeren2016] Frans H. Van Eemeren. 2016. Identifying argumentative patterns: A vital step in the development of pragma-dialectics. *Argumentation*, 30(1):1–23.

[Walton et al.2014] Douglas Walton, Alice Toniolo, and Timothy J. Norman. 2014. Missing phases of deliberation dialogue for real applications. In *Proceedings of the 11th International Workshop on Argumentation in Multi-Agent Systems*, pages 1–20.

The Good, the Bad, and the Disagreement:
Complex ground truth in rhetorical structure analysis

Debopam Das
Dept. of Linguistics
University of Potsdam
Potsdam, Germany
debdas@uni-potsdam.de

Maite Taboada
Dept. of Linguistics
Simon Fraser University
Burnaby, BC, Canada
mtaboada@sfu.ca

Manfred Stede
Dept. of Linguistics
University of Potsdam
Potsdam, Germany
stede@uni-potsdam.de

Abstract

We present a proposal to analyze disagreement in Rhetorical Structure Theory annotation which takes into account what we consider "legitimate" disagreements. In rhetorical analysis, as in many other pragmatic annotation tasks, a certain amount of disagreement is to be expected, and it is important to distinguish true mistakes from legitimate disagreements due to different possible interpretations of the structure and intention of a text. Using different sets of annotations in German and English, we present an analysis of such possible disagreements, and propose an underspecified representation that captures the disagreements.

1 Introduction

The past ten years have seen continuous interest in RST-oriented discourse parsing, which aims at automatically deriving a complete and well-formed tree representation over coherence relations assigned to adjacent spans of text. For various downstream applications (e.g., summarization, essay scoring), such a complete structure is more useful than the purely localized assignment of individual relations, as it is done in PDTB-style analysis (Prasad et al., 2008).

At the same time, it is well known that RST parsing is difficult, and furthermore, it is more difficult to achieve good human agreement on RST trees, as compared to PDTB annotation. This latter problem has not been in the spotlight of attention, though, while the computational linguistics community developed a series of parsing approaches over the years (Hernault et al., 2010; Ji and Eisenstein, 2013; Feng and Hirst, 2014; Braud et al., 2016). Part of the reason for the focus on data-

oriented automatic parsing is the availability of the RST Discourse Treebank (Carlson et al., 2003), a corpus large enough to supply training/test data in supervised machine learning (ML).

The central thesis of our paper is that the fundamental questions of RST annotation and agreement deserve to be re-opened. With powerful ML and parsing technology in place, it is timely to give more attention to the nature of the underlying data, and to its descriptive and theoretical adequacy. Our claim is that the "single ground truth asssumption" is essentially invalid for an annotation task such as rhetorical structure, which inevitably includes a fair amount of subjective decisions on the part of the annotator. As we will emphasize later, we regard this *not* as a fault of Rhetorical Structure Theory (Mann and Thompson, 1988; Taboada and Mann, 2006), but as a reality to accept, shared with labelling of other pragmatic phenomena, such as speech acts or presuppositions.

Specifically, we will argue that a certain amount of ambiguity is to be regarded as part of the "gold standard" or "ground truth". At the same time, it is clear that RST annotation is not a matter of "anything goes". So, the central challenge in our view is to differentiate between good and bad disagreement: Two annotators may legitimately disagree on some part of the analysis, when both alternatives are in line with the annotation guidelines, and they arise from, for instance, different background knowledge. This needs to be kept separate from disagreement with a not-so-well-educated annotator who misread the guidelines and thus sometimes makes analysis decisions that should not be regarded as legitimate.

Our overall project has two parts: Teasing apart the two types of disagreement, and adequately representing the space of legitimate alternative analyses. In this paper we focus on the first task and

Proceedings of the 6th Workshop Recent Advances in RST and Related Formalisms, pages 11–19,
Santiago de Compostela, Spain, September 4 2017. ©2017 Association for Computational Linguistics

provide a brief sketch of the second.

In the next section, we discuss relevant related work, and then present two agreement studies we undertook on German and English texts (Section 3). We draw conclusions from both in Section 4 and then sketch our framework for technically representing alternative analyses in Section 5. A brief summary (Section 6) concludes the paper.

2 Related work

In Computational Linguistics, a discussion on ambiguity in RST started shortly after Mann and Thompson (1988) was published, mostly in the Natural Language Generation community. The well-known proposal by Moore and Pollack (1992) argued that certain text passages can systematically have two different analyses, one drawing on the intentional, the other on the subject-matter (informational) subset of coherence relations. In a pair of two sentences, for example, when the first states a subjective claim, the second might be interpreted as EVIDENCE for the first, or as merely providing ELABORATION. Moore and Pollack also gave examples where the alternative analyses coincide with conflicting nuclearity assignments.

These questions were never really resolved; instead, with the availability of the RST Discourse Treebank (RST-DT), attention shifted to automatic parsing with ML techniques, starting with Marcu (2000), who also suggested a way of measuring agreement between competing analyses, splitting the overall task into four subtasks (units, spans, nuclearity, relations); we will also use this approach below in our experiments. As to the results achieved, Carlson et al. (2003) reported these kappa results for an experiment with pre-segmented text (i.e., where there is no point in computing unit agreement): spans .93, nuclearity .88, and relations .79. Note that these results were obtained after annotators had already worked for several months on many texts.

More recently, van der Vliet et al. (2011) annotated a Dutch corpus, and computed agreement following Marcu's method, also using pre-segmented text. They report an average kappa agreement of .88 on spans, .82 on nuclearity, and .57 for relations. These figures should not be directly compared to those of Carlson et al., because there are differences in the relation set, the guidelines, and the amount of annotator training.

The problem of ambiguity was again studied by Schilder (2002), who worked in the framework of Segmented Discourse Representation Theory or SDRT (Asher and Lascarides, 2003) and approached the problem from a semantic viewpoint. He proposed that certain aspects of the analysis could be left unannotated. For instance, nuclearity may be assigned, but the specific relation between nucleus and satellite may be left blank, if a decision cannot be reached.

Around the same time, Reitter and Stede (2003) proposed the Underspecified Rhetorical Markup Language (URML), an XML language for encoding competing analyses in a single representation. We will describe this in more detail in Section 5.

More recently, Iruskieta et al. (2015) proposed a qualitative method for analysis comparison, teasing apart constituency, relation, and attachment. The most important aspect of their comparison method is that nuclearity and relation label are separated, unlike in Marcu's quantitative agreement metric.

3 Empirical studies

Both of our studies are attached to existing RST-annotated corpora, so that our results can be related to the earlier work. Also, we used nearly-identical annotation guidelines, which we describe first, before we turn to the actual experiments.

3.1 Annotation guidelines

In contrast to the RST-DT project of Carlson et al. (2003), our annotation guidelines follow the original RST paper (Mann and Thompson, 1988) relatively closely. This means that our relation set is much smaller than that of the RST-DT (31 relations instead of 78). We do not use the many nucleus-satellite variants, and we deliberately left out suggestions like TOPIC-COMMENT or ATTRIBUTION, which we do not regard as coherence relations in the same way as those of "classic" RST.[1] We group the relations in a slightly different way from Mann & Thompson into subject-matter and presentational ones, and we have an extra category for textual relations (LIST, SUMMARY).

For technical reasons, at the moment we avoid the SAME UNIT relation of the RST DT by not

---

[1] We are of course not claiming that phenomena of Topic/Comment and Attribution do not exist. Instead, notions of information structure in our view belong to a separate level of analysis—not to that of coherence relations.

separating center-embedded segments. This decision may be revised later, and it is not critical for the purposes of this paper.

For the German experiment, we used the annotation guidelines developed for the Potsdam Commentary Corpus (Stede, 2016) and which are publicly available. Then, for annotating the English texts, we produced an English version of those guidelines and made minimal changes to the descriptions of relations (clarifications on how to distinguish between certain contrastive and argumentative relations). Further, we used language-specific segmentation guidelines that we borrowed from the implementation of SLSeg (syntactic and lexically based discourse segmenter) (Tofiloski et al., 2009).[2] In addition to many individual examples for the relations, the guidelines finish with a sample analysis of a complete text with 14 elementary discourse units (EDUs).

The guidelines merely guide the annotators in their task. They could in principle be written in such a way as to "strongly encourage" agreement when cases of ambiguity arise (e.g., by specifying preference hierarchies), but they make only minimal use of that move. The interesting issue from a theoretical viewpoint is that the same general guidelines can give rise to what we consider as legitimate disagreements.

3.2 Study I: German

For the German study (see Fodor (2015)), we selected ten texts from the publicly available Potsdam Commentary Corpus[3], which has been annotated at various levels of linguistic description, including RST. They are editorials or "pro and con" commentaries from local newspapers, with a typical length of 8 to 10 sentences (with an average length of 16 words, sentences often consist of more than one EDU). We picked texts of general-interest topics and which do not make too many references to local events or people, which might confuse annotators.

The idea of the annotation experiment was to assess the influence of the amount of training that annotators receive. Thus we worked with four annotators, all with university education. Two of them received fairly extensive training (hence-

forth: GE1 and GE2 for German Expert 1 and 2): They first read the guidelines and studied the analysis of the sample text, then discussed their questions with us. Thereafter, they were asked to individually annotate three texts (from the same genre, but not used in the experiments), and the results were jointly discussed and adjudicated. The other two annotators (henceforth: GL1 and GL2) were only lightly trained; they read the guidelines, could ask questions, and then worked on one text together, which was subsequently discussed with us. The overall procedure stretched over several days, and each annotator spent between 12 and 15 hours on the experiment. They all received €50 as reimbursement.

One variable that for present purposes we are not interested in is the segmentation of texts into EDUs. We therefore decided to present the pre segmented text (as found in the corpus) to the annotators. For one thing, this reduces the effort of the annotators, and—more importantly—it makes it easier to focus on the evaluation on the aspects we are targeting: decisions on spans, nuclearity, and relations.

In our evaluation, we first looked at the pairwise agreement of the two annotators within the groups GE1-GE2 and GL1-GL2, respectively. When applying the measures of Marcu (2000), one consequence of our using pre-segmented text needs to be discussed: Since EDUs are a priori identical for all annotators, an artificial agreement arises for the span decisions pertaining to EDUs. We decided to disregard all the spans consisting of just one EDU from the calculation. Had we included them, the overall agreement values would be higher, but the surplus would not reflect decisions made by the annotators themselves.

	Span	Nuclearity	Relation
GE1 - GE2	65.6	43.7	24.0
GL1 - GL2	51.6	25.4	9.7

Table 1: Percent agreement of annotators in the two groups (German study, 10 texts)

In this study, we calculated percent agreement among the annotators. The results for the group-internal agreement are given in Table 1. All figures are substantially better for the expert annotators, with the clearest margins for nuclearity and relations. We have to be careful in drawing conclu-

---

[2]Annotation guidelines: `http://www.sfu.ca/~mtaboada/docs/research/RST_Annotation_Guidelines.pdf`

[3]`http://angcl.ling.uni-potsdam.de/resources/pcc.html`

sions, since each group consisted of just two annotators, but the result indicates that the difference in training time and content—in particular, we surmise, the difference in the number of jointly-discussed sample analyses—leads to a marked difference in annotator agreement.

In order to measure the agreement between expert and non-expert annotators, we computed the precision and recall values for GE1 and GL1, following the method documented in Marcu (2000). GE1 was considered as the "gold" annotation. The precision and recall values, provided in Table 2, show relatively higher agreement for spans and nuclearity, but low agreement for relations. Precision and recall are the same, because there are equal numbers of false positives and false negatives.

	Precision	Recall
Span	0.65	0.65
Nuclearity	0.56	0.56
Relation	0.30	0.30

Table 2: Precision and recall for expert versus student annotation (GE1-GL1)

We also conducted various more detailed analyses, but for reasons of time, only a randomly chosen subset of five texts and their RST trees could be handled in this phase. In Table 3, we report the percent agreement results for all pairs of annotators.

	Span	Nuclearity	Relation
GE1 - GE2	63.6	43.8	27.0
GL1 - GL2	60.6	35.2	15.4
GE1 - GL1	56.6	38.8	13.2
GE1 - GL2	48.8	31.2	19.6
GE2 - GL1	63.4	44.2	23.8
GE2 - GL2	44.2	35.2	15.4

Table 3: Percent agreement of all annotator pairs (German study, 5 texts)

First of all, notice that the results for GL1-GL2 are considerably closer to those of GE1-GE2 than in the comparison of the full 10 texts; this indicates that the texts selected are "easy" ones. But the main insight to be gained from Table 3 is that the poor results of GL1-GL2 are mainly due to the performance of GL2, who consistently

reaches low agreement with all three other annotators (the single exception being the Relation agreement with GE1), while GL1 does a fairly good job; in particular s/he agrees with GE2 essentially as much as GE1 does.

One other factor we investigated is the "difficulty" of individual RST relations. On the basis of the five texts, we computed how many pairs of annotators achieve at least one perfect agreement for a particular relation type. The results are given in Table 4. The second column gives the number of pairs of annotators that agree on the relation label (and also on spans and nuclearity) in at least one text.

Relation	Ann.pairs	Percent
Preparation	6	100
Condition	6	100
Evaluation-S	5	83
List	4	66
Circumstance	4	66
Elaboration	3	50
Conjunction	3	50
Background	2	33
E-Elaboration	2	33
Contrast	2	33
Cause	2	33
Reason	1	16
Joint	1	16
Antithesis	1	16
Restatement	1	16
Result	1	16

Table 4: Pairwise annotator agreement (%) on relations (German study, 5 texts)

Again, the figures have to be taken with some caution; while the number of annotator pairs entering the calculation is not so low, we studied only five texts here. The ranking, however, confirms the intuition that those relations that tend to occur low in the tree (relating EDUs), and are often clearly marked by connectives, receive the most agreement in annotation.[4]

3.3 Study II: English

In the interest of comparability with the German study, we selected the text material from an RST-

---

[4]Running this calculation on the different levels of the hierarchy has not been done but is an interesting step for future work.

annotated corpus, in this case the RST Discourse Treebank (Carlson et al., 2003), but we did not use the associated annotation guidelines, as explained earlier. To match the genre of "commentary", we looked especially for argumentative text (which in general we expect to be more prone to competing analyses, since more interpretation and subjectivity is involved than in plain news text). In total we found 19 such documents in the RST-DT, which are letters to the editor, editorials, op-ed pieces, or reviews. For our present experiment, we selected four of the documents. One document contains multiple letters; we split it up and thus have a set of seven individual texts to work with. With an average length of 205 words per text, they are somewhat shorter than the German texts.

Also in line with the German study, we performed a pre-segmentation (following the rules mentioned in Section 3.2) of all the texts, so that annotators started from a basis that allows for a solid comparison of span, nuclearity and relation decisions. In terms of annotator teams, however, we could not exactly replicate the setting of the previous study. Instead, two authors of this paper (who have many years of experience with various RST annotation projects) served as "expert" annotators (henceforth: EE1 and EE2). On the "non-expert" side, we recruited a student of Linguistics (EL1) who carefully studied the guidelines, practiced, and discussed her questions with us. All annotations were done with RSTTool (O'Donnell, 2000).

Quantitative analysis. To determine the extent to which expertise leads to higher agreement, we again computed the percent agreement on spans, nuclearity and relations between the two experts (EE1 and EE2), and between one expert and the lightly-trained annotator (EE1 and EL1). These figures are given in Table 5. As in the German study (Table 3) we see a difference between E-E and E-L agreement, which is much less pronounced for spans than for nuclearity and relations. The main difference between the two studies, however, is that overall the English results are considerably better than the German ones. To a large extent we can attribute this to the difference in having experienced expert annotators (English) as opposed to well-trained students (German). This does not explain the better results for the EE1-EL1 pair in comparison to all the GE-GL pairs, though. There must be an additional factor,

	Span	Nuclearity	Relation
EE1 - EE2	95.1	67.0	49.8
EE1 - EL1	94.8	57.1	35.2

Table 5: Percent agreement of two annotator pairs (English study, 7 texts)

	Span	Nuclearity	Relation
EE1 - EE2	75.6	42.3	40.3
	90.2	50.5	48.2
EE1 - EL1	74.4	24.1	23.0
	89.7	35.7	33.2

Table 6: Chance-corrected agreement of two annotator pairs (English study, 7 texts); for each group, line 1 provides fixed marginal kappa, line 2 free marginal kappa

and we suspect it is the fact that the English texts are shorter and thus somewhat easier to annotate in the sense that there is less room for different interpretations.

In addition, we computed kappa values for the same pairs of annotators in order to see the influence of chance agreement. These results are shown in Table 6. In the calculations, the span agreement includes the (implicit agreement on) non-existing spans (i.e., spans that neither annotator marked), while these were left out for computing the nuclearity and relation agreement. In the related work, this point is usually not mentioned; we believe it is important to make explicit how the "virtual" spans are being handled.

Finally, as in the German study (see Table 2), we determined the agreement in terms of precision and recall between EE1 and EL1. For this purpose, we made use of RSTEval, a tool that provides precision and recall statistics between a "gold" human annotation and a parser-produced annotation.[5] EE1 was considered as the "gold" annotation here and thus we have the same scenario as in evaluations of automatic parsers against human annotations. Table 7 provides these results, showing once again high agreement in spans and nuclearity, but quite low agreement in relations. Precision and recall are the same, because there are equal numbers of false positives and false negatives.

[5]http://www.nilc.icmc.usp.br/rsteval/

	Precision	Recall
Span	0.88	0.88
Nuclearity	0.58	0.58
Relation	0.41	0.41

Table 7: Precision and recall for expert versus student annotation (EE1-EL1)

Qualitative analysis. We are also interested in a qualitative comparison: Which phenomena in the texts triggered discrepancies in the two analyses, and of what kinds are the resulting structural differences? We carried out a study of the disagreements in the English data, and found that disagreements involving spans, nuclearity and relations emerge from a number of sources. This is evident in the pairwise comparison between the expert annotations, and to a larger degree, between the expert and non-expert annotations.

Differences in spans primarily result from differences in the point of attachment of EDUs or larger segments. Figures 1 and 2 below exemplify two structures produced by the expert annotators who attach the spans at either different points or different levels. Both annotations employ CONTRAST and BACKGROUND relations, but the spans constituting these relations are different in length and hierarchy.

The situation is more complicated in cases for nuclearity where there are two main sources of disagreement. In the first case, the annotators assign equal or unequal importance to the respective spans, resulting in the formation of a mononuclear and a multinuclear relation. In the second case, both the annotators choose a mononuclear relation, but each assigns a different nucleus-satellite order (NS vs. SN order) to the respective spans.

More importantly, the differences in nuclearity assignment have a follow-up effect on choosing relevant relation labels. First, assigning a mononuclear vs. multinuclear structure further constrains the choice of relation labels, as the mononuclear and multinuclear relations in an RST taxonomy contain two mutually exclusive sets of relations. For instance, in one of our analyses, assigning equal vs. unequal importance to spans results into a mononuclear ANTITHESIS and a multinuclear CONTRAST relation (Note: both relations are of contrastive type). Second, assigning an opposite nucleus-satellite order also contributes to selecting different relations, most of which are mirror relations (differing primarily according to the nucleus-satellite order), such as CAUSE vs. RESULT.

Finally, the differences in relation are also caused by choosing an altogether different or similar relation label for the otherwise same discourse structure involving the same spans and identical nuclearity assignment. We have one such example in our corpus, with the two labels being SUMMARY and RESTATEMENT.

4 Conclusions from the experiments

The most popular method to measure agreement Marcu (2000) computes precision and recall with four factors: Elementary Discourse Units (EDUs), units linked with relations (Spans), nucleus or satellite status (Nuclearity), and relation label (Relation). One problem with this method is that it measures twice the same type of decision: Whether the units are linked (Span), and the status of each unit as nucleus or satellite. This problem is extensively discussed by Iruskieta et al. (2015).

Another problem with this type of evaluation is that it is just quantitative, that is, it does not distinguish between different types of disagreements and their "quality". We believe that on the one hand there are true mistakes in discourse annotation, maybe due to lack of experience in annotation, carelessness, or any other human factor. We also believe, however, that other differences in annotation may be considered legitimate disagreement, i.e., annotations that are both valid from a theoretical point of view. This is particularly the case in argumentative texts, where the analysis hinges on how the annotator perceives the writer's intentions. Those may not be equally clear to annotators in argumentative texts, as they are more subjective than descriptive text types.

In particular, what we find with inter-annotator agreement studies, is that (i) spans are relatively easy to identify; (ii) nuclearity increases complexity and leads to disagreements; and, most importantly, (iii) relation assignment seems particularly difficult. We propose that some of the more fine-grained distinctions among relations may not be relevant in all cases and all uses of RST trees. Thus, an underspecified representation of spans and nuclearity, plus reliably annotated relations, may be sufficient in many cases. We propose such a representation in the next section.

5 The complex gold: Capturing ambiguity

As we mentioned earlier, the second part of our overall project is to represent the expert annotations in a common data structure; in this paper, we describe the direction we are taking. Below, we briefly describe the framework we are using for this, and illustrate the conversion with an example from the English expert annotations.

5.1 URML

The Underspecified Rhetorical Markup Language (URML) was introduced by Reitter and Stede (2003) primarily to facilitate automatic RST parsing: The authors envisaged a pipeline analysis where subsequent modules can refine underspecified intermediate results of earlier modules. To some extent, this was implemented in the early SVM-based parser by Reitter (2003).

Our proposal here is that URML can serve to represent the complex ground truth derived from multiple expert annotations. In brief, URML is an XML format that regards every node of an RST tree as a data point to be described with various attributes and with elements pointing to the daughters (satellite and nucleus, or two nuclei). URML was designed to represent only binary trees, but that is in line with most existing implementations (including the RST parsers mentioned earlier), which usually work with binarized versions of the data.

An URML file for a text consists of three major blocks: an enumeration of all the RST relations in the set, a sequence of the EDUs of the text, and a sequence of node descriptions. This node-centric representation allows for *subtree sharing*: Competing analyses can be encoded to share common subtrees by referring to the same node ID. Other ways of underspecification are: (i) The name of the relation for a node can be specified or left out; as an intermediate variant, it is also possible to only state whether it is some mono- or multinuclear relation. (ii) The nucleus/satellite status of daughter nodes can be left open. (iii) The mechanism of *local ambiguity packing* allows for representations of alternative subtrees, whose root node IDs are specified to belong to the same *group*. Each relation node can also have a numerical score attribute, so that probabilities or preferences among the alternatives in a group can be encoded.

A limitation of URML lies in the fact that dependencies between different decisions cannot be represented. For example, the choice between relation R1 and R2 at node X might entail a preference for subtree S1 over S2 at one of X's daughter nodes. If such constellations need to be covered, the only way is to use alternative analyses, i.e., two (or more) complete URML graphs.[6]

5.2 Coding alternative expert trees in URML

We coded the RST trees resulting from our empirical study on the seven English texts (Section 3.3) in URML and found that all the phenomena of "legitimate disagreement" can be captured in this framework. In contrast to the original uses of URML envisaged by Reitter and Stede (2003), who focused on underspecification accompanying an incremental parsing technique, our goal here is to effectively represent genuine ambiguity. We thus make use of structure sharing and ambiguity packing, but not of unspecified relation names or types.

We demonstrate the functionality with an excerpt from one text of our study (from wsj_1117), looking at the expert annotators EE1 and EE2. For reasons of space and readability, we replaced the text segments with segment identifiers and show the two expert annotations in Figures 1 and 2. This is in fact one of the worst cases of disagreement that resulted from our study. At first sight the trees look quite different, but notice that: 1) both versions picked up a CONTRAST whose spans meet between S2 and S3; 2) both versions picked up a BACKGROUND whose spans meet between S5 and S6; and 3) the analyses for S3 – S5 are identical.

The disagreement thus amounts to the extension of the spans of the CONTRAST and BACKGROUND, the relation between S1 and S2, and the subtrees for S6 – S8. Here is an excerpt from the URML encoding of the node descriptions:

```
<parRelation id="N1a" group="N1"
    type="Contrast"
    annotator="V1"
    score="0.5">
  <nucleus id="N2a">
  <nucleus id="N5">
</parRelation>
<hypRelation id="N1b" group="N1"
 type="Background"
    annotator="V2"
    score="0.5">
  <nucleus id="N6b">
```

---

[6]For our present purposes, we did not encounter the need for this step.

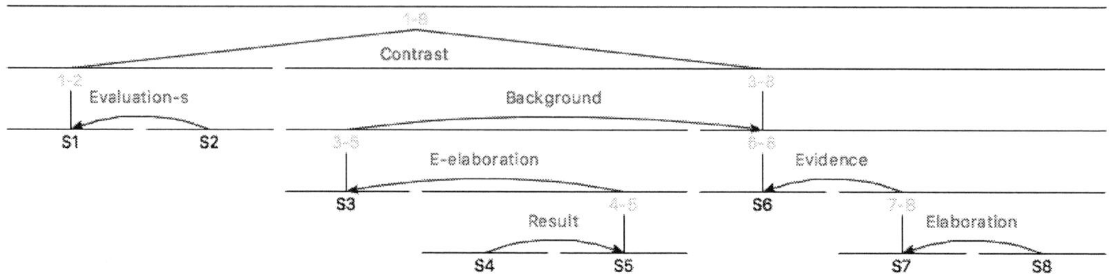

Figure 1: Annotation by EE1 for part of a corpus text (English study)

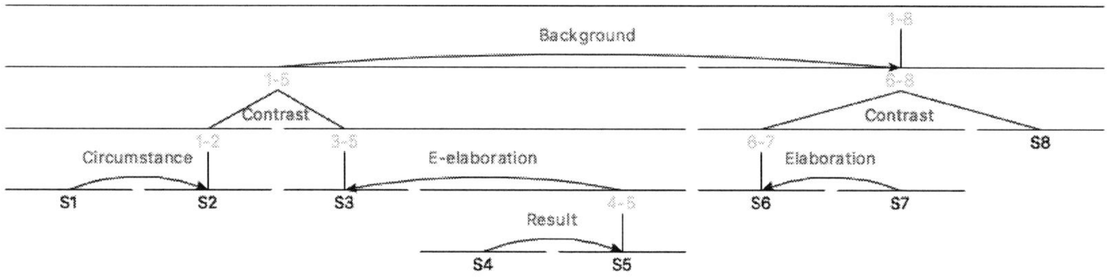

Figure 2: Annotation by EE2 for part of a corpus text (English study)

```
    <satellite id="N4">
</hypRelation>

<parRelation id="N4" type="Contrast"
    annotator="V2">
    <nucleus id="N2b">
    <nucleus id="N3">
</parRelation>
```

The declarations state that nodes N1a and N1b are alternative analyses provided by annotators EE1 and EE2. They are alternatives because they belong to the same group N1, and cover the same sequence of EDUs (S1–S8). In contrast, N4 does not belong to a group, i.e., it occurs only in EE-2's analysis. The first nucleus of both CONTRAST relations is an alternative of group N2 (not shown here), which represents the analyses for segments S1–S2.

In the same way, the other disagreements between EE1 and EE2 can be captured in the same URML representation, which thus plays the role of a "complex gold" annotation.

6 Summary

With two empirical studies, we demonstrated that annotator agreement depends on the amount of training and expertise the annotators have acquired. While this is hardly surprising, our next step is to differentiate between non-expert dis-agreement (some of which can arise from failure to adhere to the given guidelines, annotation flaws, or other human factors) and what we call "legitimate disagreement", i.e., that between expert annotators. Our proposal here is that competing expert analyses should be regarded as part of the "ground truth" in an annotated corpus. Besides differentiating between annotator expertise by means of quantitative measures, we undertook a first qualitative analysis of the types of disagreements encountered among experts. In future work, this needs to be elaborated.

The second point we made is that we can use the URML representation framework (which had originally been designed for a somewhat different purpose) to capture the disagreement in annotations in a single representation for a text. Our initial result is that the analyses used in the English study could all be mapped to URML and adequately represent the alternatives in the annotations. Here, the next step for us is to provide tools for automatic mapping (and merging) from the rs3 format of RSTTool to URML, and to devise ways of computing annotator agreement between a "new" annotator, or an RST parser for that matter, and the URML graph representing the "complex gold".

References

Nicholas Asher and Alex Lascarides. 2003. *Logics of Conversation*. Cambridge University Press, Cambridge.

Chloé Braud, Barbara Plank, and Anders Søgaard. 2016. Multi-view and multi-task training of RST discourse parsers. In *Proceedings of the 26th International Conference on Computational Linguistics (COLING)*. Osaka, Japan, pages 1903–1913.

Lynn Carlson, Daniel Marcu, and Mary Ellen Okurowski. 2003. Building a discourse-tagged corpus in the framework of Rhetorical Structure Theory. In Jan van Kuppevelt and Ronnie Smith, editors, *Current Directions in Discourse and Dialogue*, Kluwer, Dordrecht, pages 85–112.

Vanessa Wei Feng and Graeme Hirst. 2014. A linear-time bottom-up discourse parser with constraints and post-editing. In *Proceedings of the 52nd Annual Meeting of the Association for Computational Linguistics*. Baltimore, MA, pages 511–521.

Iskra Fodor. 2015. *Übereinstimmung zwischen Annotatoren als Ähnlichkeitsmaß für RST-Bäume-Eine empirische Studie mit Texten aus dem Potsdam Commentary Corpus*. B.Sc. Thesis, University of Potsdam.

Hugo Hernault, Hemut Prendinger, David duVerle, and Mitsuru Ishizuka. 2010. Hilda: A discourse parser using support vector machine classification. *Dialogue and Discourse* 1(3):1–33.

Mikel Iruskieta, Iria da Cunha, and Maite Taboada. 2015. Principles of a qualitative method for rhetorical analysis evaluation: A contrastive analysis english-spanish-basque. *Language Resources and Evaluation* 49(2):263–309.

Yangfeng Ji and Jacob Eisenstein. 2013. Discriminative improvements to distributional sentence similarity. In *Proceedings of the 2013 Conference on Empirical Methods in Natural Language Processing*. Association for Computational Linguistics, Seattle, Washington, USA, pages 891–896.

William Mann and Sandra Thompson. 1988. Rhetorical Structure Theory: Towards a functional theory of text organization. *Text* 8:243–281.

Daniel Marcu. 2000. *The theory and practice of discourse parsing and summarization*. MIT Press, Cambridge/MA.

Johanna Moore and Martha Pollack. 1992. A problem for RST: The need for multi-level discourse analysis. *Computational Linguistics* 18(4):537–544.

Michael O'Donnell. 2000. RSTTool 2.4 – A markup tool for Rhetorical Structure Theory. In *Proc. of the International Natural Language Generation Conference*. Mizpe Ramon/Israel, pages 253–256.

Rashmi Prasad, Nikhil Dinesh, Alan Lee, Eleni Miltsakaki, Livio Robaldo, Aravind Joshi, and Bonnie Webber. 2008. The Penn Discourse Treebank 2.0. In *Proc. of the 6th International Conference on Language Resources and Evaluation (LREC)*. Marrakech, Morocco.

David Reitter. 2003. Simple signals for complex rhetorics: On rhetorical analysis with rich-feature support vector models. *LDV Forum* 18(1/2):38–52.

David Reitter and Manfred Stede. 2003. Step by step: underspecified markup in incremental rhetorical analysis. In *Proceedings of the 4th International Workshop on Linguistically Interpreted Corpora (LINC)*. Budapest.

Frank Schilder. 2002. Robust discourse parsing via discourse markers, topicality and position. *Natural Language Engineering* 8(2-3):235–255.

Manfred Stede. 2016. Rhetorische Struktur. In Manfred Stede, editor, *Handbuch Textannotation: Potsdamer Kommentarkorpus 2.0*, Universitätsverlag, Potsdam.

Maite Taboada and William Mann. 2006. Rhetorical Structure Theory: Looking back and moving ahead. *Discourse Studies* 8(4):423–459.

Milan Tofiloski, Julian Brooke, and Maite Taboada. 2009. A syntactic and lexical-based discourse segmenter. In *Proceedings of the Joint Conference of the 47th Annual Meeting of the ACL and the 4th International Joint Conference on Natural Language Processing of the AFNLP (Short Papers)*. Suntec, Singapore, pages 77–80.

Nynke van der Vliet, Ildikó Berzlánovich, Gosse Bouma, Markus Egg, and Gisela Redeker. 2011. Building a discourse-annotated Dutch text corpus. In *Proceedings of the Workshop Beyond Semantics: Corpus-based annotations of Pragmatics and Discourse Phenomena*. Göttingen, Germany, pages 157–171.

A Distributional View of Discourse Encapsulation:
Multifactorial Prediction of Coreference Density in RST

Amir Zeldes

Department of Linguistics, Georgetown University
`amir.zeldes@georgetown.edu`

Abstract

Early formulations of discourse coherence constraints postulated a connection between coreference likelihood and distance within a discourse parse, e.g. in the framework of Veins Theory (Cristea et al. 1998%CristeaIdeRomary1998), which proposes that coreference is expected to be encapsulated within tightly linked areas of discourse parses, called Domains of Referential Accessibility (DRAs). Using an RST dependency representation, this paper expands on previous work showing the relevance of DRAs to coreference likelihood. We develop a multifactorial model using both rhetorical and surface distance metrics, as well as confounds such as unit length and genre, and direct versus indirect rhetorical paths. We also explore coreferential accessibility as it applies to less studied types of coreference, including bridging and lexical coreference. The results show that rhetorical and surface distance, as well as direct linking, all influence coreference likelihood, and should not be treated as mutually exclusive or redundant metrics. Finally, we incorporate RST relation-specific tendencies that offer a more fine-grained model of coreference accessibility.

1 Introduction

Accessibility of discourse referents has been a major theme in discourse parsing frameworks since the beginning of the field. Polanyi (1988:616)%Polanyi1988 suggested that the stack of discourse units determined which discourse referents were available to be pronominalized; in Segmented Discourse Representation Theory (SDRT), the Right Frontier Constraint (Asher 1993%Asher1993) posited that newly attached discourse units could only link to the previous or immediately dominating segment, and later that anaphora was restricted to this domain (see Asher & Lascarides 2003%AsherLascarides2003); and in Rhetorical Structure Theory (RST, Mann & Thompson 1988%MannThompson1988), Veins Theory (Cristea et al. 1998%CristeaIdeRomary1998) was developed to identify Domains of Referential Accessibility (DRAs), said to constrain coreference relations. We can refer to the conjecture behind these approaches as the 'Discourse Encapsulation Hypothesis' (DEH), i.e. that discourse structure constrains domains of co-referentiality.

Empirical work examining different forms of the DEH has primarily focused on showing that some kind of discourse distance metric or domain definition is superior to surface distance as a predictor of coreferentiality, or to some other proposed metrics (e.g. Cristea et al. 1999%CristeaIdeMarcuEtAl1999, Tetreault & Allen 2003%TetreaultAllen2003, Chiarcos & Krasavina 2008%ChiarcosKrasavina2008). Surprisingly, there seems to be no work suggesting that rather than comparing DRA definitions to surface distance definitions, we could attempt to combine them, or even pool further predictors into a multifactorial model of coreferential accessibility – this will be the main goal of the present paper.

The idea that a multifactorial model may be more useful than categorical definitions of accessi-

Proceedings of the 6th Workshop Recent Advances in RST and Related Formalisms, pages 20–28,
Santiago de Compostela, Spain, September 4 2017. ©2017 Association for Computational Linguistics

ble domains gains credence from recent advances in the use machine learning for discourse annotation. While using cues from discourse parsing is still not standard in state of the art coreference resolution systems (Durret & Klein 2014%DurrettKlein2014, Clark & Manning 2015%ClarkManning2015, Wiseman et al. 2016%WisemanRushShieber2016), recent work in discourse parsing suggests that knowing about coreference can improve RST parsers (Surdeanu et al. 2015%SurdeanuEtAl2015, Braud et al. 2016%BraudPlankSoegaard2016), RST-based sentence compression (Durrett et al. 2016%DurrettBerg-KirkpatrickKlein2016), and discourse cohesion metrics (Iida & Tokunaga 2012%IidaTokunaga2012).

Different frameworks have applied some kind of DEH to different types of coreference: pronominal anaphora only (e.g. Tetreault & Allen 2003%TetreaultAllen2003, Chiarcos & Krasavina 2008%ChiarcosKrasavina2008), also lexical coreference (Cristea et al. 1999%CristeaIdeMarcuEtAl1999), or specific phenomena (e.g. discourse deictic and demonstrative *this/that*, Webber 1991%Webber1991). These approaches are in principle testable for any type of referentiality, and this paper will therefore compare coreference at large, pronominal anaphora, and bridging anaphora (Asher & Lascarides 1998%AsherLascarides1998).

Finally, previous approaches have explicitly disregarded the role of discourse function labels and utterance types in predicting coreferentiality domains, despite the relatively plausible proposition that certain relations or combinations of relations may influence coreference likelihood (e.g. we would expect coreference within an RST *Restatement*, but *Purpose* satellites may be less likely to co-refer to entities in their nuclei). In fact, many discourse connectives which signal specific relations have anaphoric components, e.g. causal connectives such as *therefore*, which imply event anaphora (see Stede & Grishina 2016%StedeGrishina2016).

In order to construct a multifactorial model of referent accessibility for coreference, anaphora and bridging, in Section 2 we present the data and scope of annotations used in this study. We then argue for the use of a dependency representation of RST, rather than traditional constituent trees for this task. Section 3 discusses the operationalization of discourse distance and the features used in our model, followed by the results in Section 4, and concluding with some discussion in Section 5.

2 Data

2.1 The GUM corpus

To model the DEH, we need data that is annotated for both RST and coreference, which narrows down the possible choices of corpus. The first natural choice for an RST corpus would normally have been the RST Discourse Treebank (Carlson et al. 2001%CarlsonEtAl2001), the largest available RST corpus, parts of which overlap with the coreference annotated portion of OntoNotes (Hovy et al. 2006%HovyMarcusPalmerEtAl2006). Although coreference annotations are available for 182 of the 380 Wall Street Journal documents in the RST Discourse Treebank (RSTDT), using OntoNotes coreference data to test the DEH is problematic, since OntoNotes rules out indefinite NPs as possible anaphors, as well as a variety of special situations, the most relevant of which are illustrated in (1)-(4) (all examples are from OntoNotes, but none are annotated as coreferent there).

(1) **Indefinite/generic:** [*Program trading*] *is "a racket,"* ... [*program trading*] *creates ... swings*
(2) **Modifiers nouns:** *small investors seem to be adapting to greater* [*stock market*] *volatility ... Glenn Britta ... is "factoring"* [*the market's*] *volatility "into investment decisions."*
(3) **Metonymy:** *a strict interpretation ... requires* [*the U.S.*] *to notify foreign dictators of certain coup plots ...* [*Washington*] *rejected the bid ...*
(4) **Nesting:** *He has in tow* [*his prescient girl friend, whose sassy retorts mark* [*her*] *...*]

Another phenomenon of interest that is not covered by OntoNotes data is bridging (see Asher & Lascarides 1998%AsherLascarides1998), shown in example (5), which will be evaluated separately in Section 4.

(5) *Mexico's President Salinas said* [*the country*]*'s recession had ended and* [*the economy*] *was growing again.*

In order to include these phenomena, we use the GUM corpus, containing 76 documents (64,000 tokens) in four genres of English from the Web (news, interviews, how-to guides and travel guides) annotated for RST, coreference, entities, syntax and a variety of other annotations (see Zeldes 2016%Zeldes2016).[1] The RST analyses in GUM use a fairly small, high-level inventory of 20 relations similar to the RSTDT's 16 top-level relation classes (see Section 4.3), while coreference relations cover 5 types: anaphora, cataphora (forward-pointing link), lexical coreference, apposition and bridging.

2.2 Rhetorical Structure Dependencies

In order to evaluate the DEH, we need to operationalize the notion of Rhetorical Distance (RD) in an RST graph. Here the argument will be presented that a 'flat' dependency-like structure offers a more intuitive way of calculating distances than fully hierarchical RST trees.

Because RST instantiates non-terminal nodes (spans and 'multinucs', i.e. multinuclear units), a direct comparison of surface distance and 'rhetorical distance' between elementary discourse units (EDUs) is non-trivial. An intuitive approach might be to count edges along the path between two EDUs, including transitions to non-terminal nodes (see Chiarcos & Krasavina 2008%ChiarcosKrasavina2008 for discussion). In this case, the RD between [1] and [3] in Figure 1 would be 3, which we write as *RD(u1,u3)=3*. However, there are both practical and theoretical problems with this way of counting.

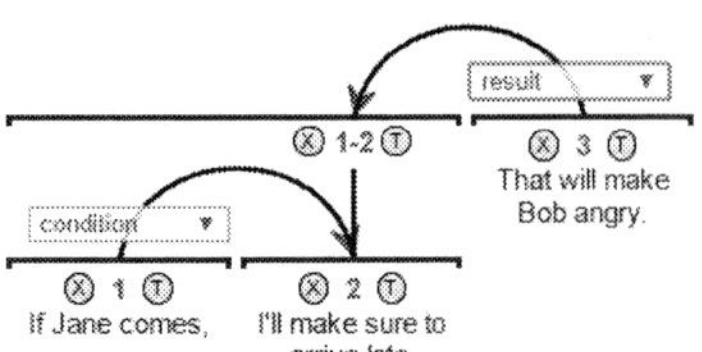

Figure 1. A simple RST example with a non-terminal span. *RD(u1,u3)=3* and *RD(u2,u3)=2*.

From a practical perspective, we note that *RD(u2,u3)=2*; this measurement is a direct result of the presence of the span [1-2], which is only

<hr>

needed due to the conditional in [1]. For the same two units with the same relation, *RD=1* in Figure 2.

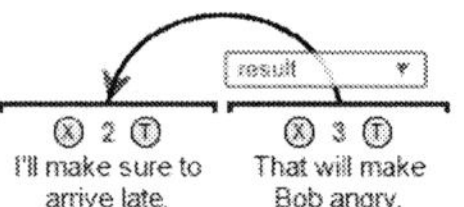

Figure 2. Without the conditional EDU, *RD(u2,u3)=1*.

This behavior is counter-intuitive, since for purposes of coreference likelihood, we would like to say that the rhetorical cohesion of the predicates in [2] and [3] is direct: Bob being angry in [3] is the result of arriving late in [2]. At least from a coreference-centric perspective, there is no reason to assume less tight juncture between referents in [2] and [3] due to having a further satellite to the left.

From a more theoretical standpoint, assuming equal distance regardless of the presence of peripheral modifiers is consistent with Marcu's (1996)%Marcu1996 compositionality criterion for discourse trees, which posits that 'spans can be joined in a larger span by a given rhetorical relation if and only if that relation holds also between the most salient units of those spans' (Marcu 1996:1070%Marcu1996; see also Zhang & Liu 2016%ZhangLiu2016 for an empirical study).

For these reasons, the present paper uses a conversion of the RST data from the GUM corpus into a dependency-style format, which contains no non-terminal nodes, linking only EDUs to each other such that relations emanating from spans are represented by edges linked to their nuclei. Several dependency representations have recently been suggested for RST, most notably by Hirao et al. (2013)%HiraoYoshidaNishinoEtAl2013 and Li et al. (2014)%LiWangCaoEtAl2014. A key difference between these representations is the handling of multinuclear relations (see Hayashi et al. 2016%HayashiHiraoNagata2016 for comparison and discussion). Figure 3, reproduced from Hayashi et al., illustrates the two approaches, which roughly correspond to propagating a multinuc's outgoing relation to its children, or using the multinuc relation name to connect its children. In this paper we follow Li et al.'s approach, which allows us to retain information about multinuclear relations (this will become important in Section 4).

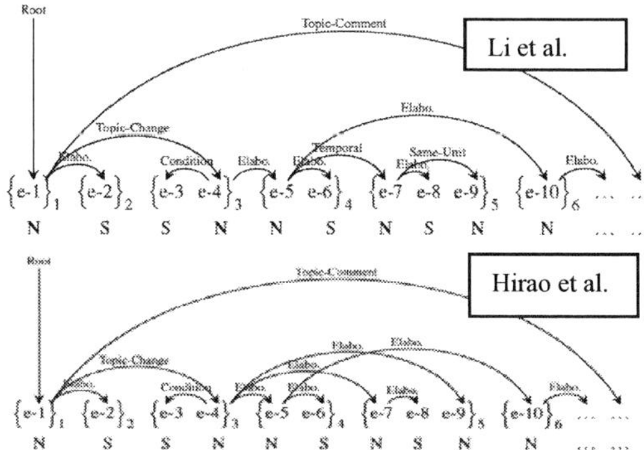

Figure 3. Rhetorical Structure Dependency representations (reproduced from Hayashi et al. 2016)

Using a dependency representation of the GUM data, calculating RD is simple, and hierarchy depth issues are avoided.[2] A limitation of this approach is that we no longer have access to the relative linking order of satellites: we could want to consider more closely nested satellites to be closer. For example, in the top representation in Figure 3, *RD(e-1,e-2) = RD(e-1,e-4) = 1*. If the tree allows crossing edges, we no longer know whether e-2 or e-4 are more closely linked to e-1. Although Marcu's compositionality criterion suggests that this difference should be irrelevant, we reserve the possibility of RD metrics incorporating nesting depth in some way for future work; in any event, it seems reasonable that both *RD(e-1,e-2)* and *RD(e-1,e-4)* should be greater than *RD(e-1,e-3)*, and this assumption is respected by the suggested representation.

3 Setup

3.1 Operationalization

The dependent variable of interest in this study is the degree of coreferentiality between EDUs, but there are multiple ways of considering whether/to what extent coreference holds between any two units. One decision is whether coreferentiality constitutes binary (some coreference detected) or count data (how many coreferent entities, or entity mentions). Although more categorical formulations

of the DEH may evoke interest in the binary option, a realistic corpus approach means expecting a range of different densities of coreferentiality at all distances, so that ignoring frequencies seems like an undesirable loss of information. We therefore choose to focus on count data modeling coreference density (but see Section 4.3 on binary prediction).

A second important distinction is whether we are interested in immediate antecedents or simply any members of a coreference chain. Clearly as distance grows, the immediate antecedent of an entity mention becomes unlikely across a pair of EDUs; however, distant EDUs may still discuss the same referents, which we will detect if we consider any distance in the coreference chain as an instance of the target phenomenon. As it is not clear which of these formulations is most interesting, we will tentatively examine both and compare the results in Section 4.

3.2 Features

Our dataset covers all possible pairs of EDUs within the same document in each of the documents in GUM. The corpus contains 4788 EDUs in 76 documents, which produce over 170K distinct EDU pairs. For each pair we collect:

- Name and genre of the document
- Surface distance in EDUs
- RD based on dependency representation
- Length in tokens
- Rough sentence type (10 types available in GUM, e.g. declarative, imperative, question, fragment..)
- Direct ancestry – a binary variable, whether one EDU is a direct ancestor of the other in the dependency tree
- Outgoing RST relation name
- Head POS and grammatical function
- Whether or not the EDU is a subordinate clause (values: attached left, right or none)
- Amount of coreferent mentions across the pair (excluding bridging; see below)
- Amount of direct antecedent relations across the pair (excluding bridging)
- The latter metric, but only for bridging

---

[2] Code generating the dependency representation from .rs3 files is available from `https://github.com/amir-zeldes/rst2dep`. The data itself is available from the GUM website.

Since bridging is not a transitive relation, we do not collect information about indirect chains containing a bridging link.

While collecting the count of direct antecedents is fairly straight-forward, computing indirect coreference is more complex. If, for example, an entity is mentioned twice in an EDU and once in a preceding EDU, we need to decide whether the coreference count is 1 or 2. Note that while each of the two mentions in the later EDU has an indirect antecedent in the earlier EDU, there is only one coreferent entity. However, collapsing the multiple mentions in an EDU means losing information – on some level, it makes intuitive sense that multiple subsequent mentions of the same entity should count as realizing an increase in cohesion. In the evaluation below, we therefore do not collapse multiple mentions and concentrate on *coreference density* as the metric for indirect coreferentiality. For direct antecedents and bridging, this issue does not arise: entity and mention density are the same.

4 Results

4.1 Coreference

Direct antecedent coreferentiality is a comparatively sparse phenomenon: in permuting all possible EDU pairs for the evaluation, very few mentions have their direct antecedent in any given pair, with the range in our data spanning only 0-6 coreferent mentions. At the same time, it is also highly correlated with EDU distance: direct antecedents are usually quite close to their present mention. Indirect coreference, by contrast, can be spread out throughout documents, and is much more frequent: while most EDUs share fewer than 4 mentions in common, outlier cases can have as many as 34 mentions in common (by repeating several identical mentions multiple times, usually only possible in longer EDUs). Figure 4 gives an overview of the relationship between EDU distance (bottom) or RD (top) and direct coreference (right) or indirect coreference (left).

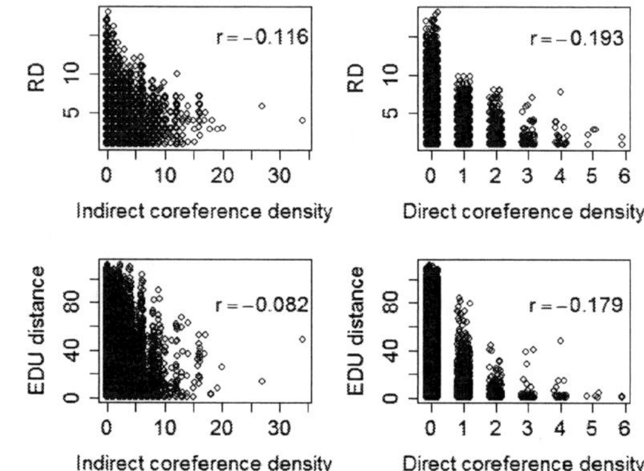

Figure 4. Direct and indirect coreference density as a function of EDU distance and RD.

As the correlation coefficients in the plots show, coreference is negatively correlated with distance in all cases; however for both direct and indirect density, RD is slightly more correlated than EDU surface distance. At the same time it should be noted that EDU distance and RD are significantly correlated ($r = 0.243$, $p < 2.2e-16$), and that high coreference density is in most cases connected to sentence length as well, since longer EDUs have a higher chance of matching multiple mentions. It is therefore difficult to evaluate the DEH without a multifactorial view of the data.

To address these confounds, we perform a linear mixed effects Poisson regression using the lme4 package in R, modelling the approximate shape of coreference density.[3] As fixed effects we initially consider EDU distance, RD, and EDU length of both units (z-score transformed). We also add two further predictors: the genre a document comes from and direct ancestry between the EDUs. Ancestry can be important, since RD does not capture an important distinction in measuring 'encapsulation': intuitively, a direct RST ancestor is more tightly connected to an RST child than units for which we must go 'up the tree and back down', even if the number of edges in both cases is identical. Genre is not strictly necessary, but it may be reasonable to assume that coreference likelihood and RD distance patterns vary systematically

---

[3] The Poisson distribution is a good fit for the left bounded distribution of coreference density bands: values under 0 are not possible, and the expected value is between 0 and 1 (I thank an anonymous reviewer for commenting on this).

across the genres represented in our data. Document identity is treated as a random effect introducing idiosyncratic noise into the data. Model coefficients are given below first for direct coreference.

```
Random effects:
 Groups Name         Variance Std.Dev.
  doc    (Intercept) 0.01434  0.1197
Number of obs: 172150, groups: doc, 76

Fixed effects:
             Estimate Std. Error z value Pr(>|z|)
(Intercept) -0.579493   0.056438  -10.27   <2e-16 ***
scale(len1)  0.221689   0.009478   23.39   <2e-16 ***
scale(len2)  0.193865   0.009436   20.55   <2e-16 ***
rsd_dist    -0.332126   0.012633  -26.29   <2e-16 ***
edu_dist    -0.139895   0.002778  -50.36   <2e-16 ***
genrenews   -0.056477   0.053785   -1.05   0.2937
genrevoyage -0.486155   0.056290   -8.64   <2e-16 ***
genrewhow   -0.096990   0.051096   -1.90   0.0577 .
directTrue   0.380319   0.035008   10.86   <2e-16 ***
---
p-val. 0 '***' 0.001 '**' 0.01 '*' 0.05 '.' 0.1 ' ' 1
```

The model shows that all of the relevant predictors are highly significant: even knowing both EDU lengths (which are clearly very important), as well as RD and EDU distance, and direct ancestry too, all predictors remain highly useful. Genre, by contrast, is less important, with only the travel guide genre (voyage) being associated with a lower coreferentiality baseline.

Looking at model coefficients, we see that length is likely to outweigh distance metrics in effect size as long as distance is moderate: an increase of one z-score in sentence length above the mean is associated with increases of about 0.2 coreferent mentions. Each EDU distance unit, by contrast, decreases coreferentiality by about 0.13 units compared to the intercept, which can however mount up. RD units have a stronger effect per unit (0.33), but a lower z value (-26 for RD, but -50 for EDU distance). This is understandable since for direct coreferentiality, distance can become overwhelming, and even units mentioning the same entities can score 0 due to the direct antecedent being elsewhere. Finally, being a direct ancestor (no going up and down the RST tree) offsets more than one unit of RD, suggesting that this relationship has a substantial effect. The overall model fit measured in r^2 for the correlation of fitted and actual values is 0.19, a respectable value considering we are predicting degree of coreferentiality without knowing anything about the contents of the EDUs; in other words, the model accounts for about a fifth of the variance in coreference density.

We can now compare the results above to what happens when we model indirect coreference, using the same predictors. In order for the model not to be skewed by comparatively rare outliers with over 15 coreferent mention pairs, the dependent variable in this case will be z-score scaled and fitted to a Gaussian distribution. Although the Gaussian model t-values cannot be translated into p-values directly due to inexact degrees of freedom (see Baayen 2008:269%Baayen2008), a conservative estimate treats values more extreme than ± 2 as significant.

```
Random effects:
 Groups    Name        Variance Std.Dev.
  doc       (Intercept) 0.09789  0.3129
  Residual              0.82965  0.9109
Number of obs: 172150, groups: doc, 76

Fixed effects:
              Estimate Std. Error t value
(Intercept)  0.2695836  0.0723038    3.73
scale(len1)  0.2043943  0.0023432   87.23
scale(len2)  0.1833124  0.0023811   76.99
rsd_dist    -0.0511588  0.0014351  -35.65
edu_dist    -0.0015377  0.0001168  -13.17
genrenews   -0.0348780  0.0997936   -0.35
genrevoyage -0.2161897  0.1047555   -2.06
genrewhow    0.0969725  0.1016942    0.95
directTrue   0.2280120  0.0091334   24.96
```

Again, genre is not a strong predictor, with 'voyage' somewhat below the intercept. Sentence lengths are now even more significant (largest t-values), and effect sizes per z-score unit are much larger than for the distance metrics. However the most interesting part of the result is the disparity between the very weak (but significant) effect of EDU distance, compared to a 50 times more influential contribution of RD. An RD shift of four units is as strong as a standard deviation in sentence length, but EDU shifts needs to be more than 10 times as large for the same effect. This suggests that a large part of the effect found for the direct model simply reflects the proximity of immediate antecedents. Finally, direct ancestry still plays a role, comparable to just over one standard deviation in EDU length. The total model r^2 is 0.17, a slightly worse fit, but unsurprising considering the reduced informativity of surface distance.

4.2 Bridging and pronominal anaphora

Following the results for coreference at large, we can also ask whether bridging and pronominal anaphora pattern in the same way. From a discourse cohesion point of view, bridging is a very similar phenomenon to coreference, since resolving bridging reference requires recourse to antecedents. Due to the non-transitive nature of the relation, the distribution is very sparse: Only 601 out of over 170,000 possible EDU pairs exhibit some bridging (one or more cases). This highly skewed distribution makes a regression on the complete dataset problematic: even if we cast the problem as binomial (bridging present or absent), the regression will inevitably learn to guess 'no bridging', a majority baseline which achieves over 99% accuracy. For bridging we therefore opt to concentrate on the distribution of those pairs that do exhibit some bridging. Figure 5 shows a log-log scatter plot of RD and EDU distance for bridging cases, distinguishing direct and indirect rhetorical dominance paths. Each circle represents an EDU pair, with circle size corresponding to the number of bridging instances for that pair.

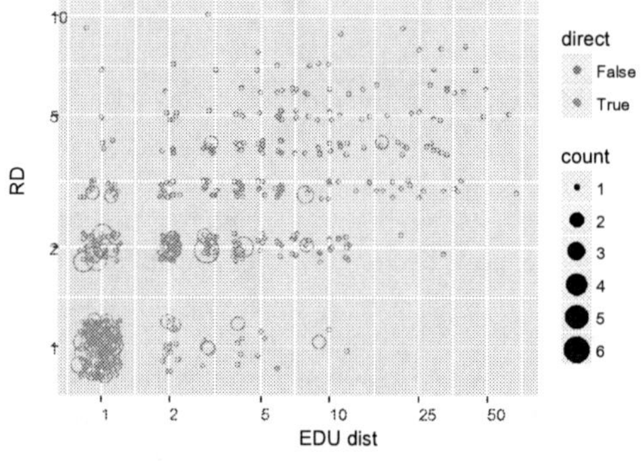

Figure 5. RD vs. EDU distance for pairs with bridging, also showing direct rhetorical ancestry (log-log scale).

The figure shows that most of the data has immediate proximity ($RD=ED=1$, 30.2% of pairs, covering 32.1% of bridging cases). However much like for coreference, bridging covers a wide range of EDU distances, and remains somewhat well attested at range: the mean EDU distance is 5.27 (comparable to direct coreference: 5.23), whereas RD, which only reaches 10, is strongly concentrated in the region below 4 or 5, with a mean of $RD=2.45$ (a small, but significant difference to direct coreference: 2.62).

Long-distance direct ancestry is unsurprisingly rare, especially for high RD, and cases are concentrated at the bottom of the plot. However the preponderance of direct ancestry in bridging cases is particularly high: 45.7% of EDU pairs exhibiting

bridging are in a rhetorical ancestry relation, covering 48% of bridging instances. By contrast, 43.2% of direct coreference EDU pairs (and 45.7% of coreference instances) have direct ancestry, and a much lower 14.3% and 15.6% respectively for indirect coreference. In sum, it seems that while bridging is too rare to build a complete multifactorial model, it has similar distance and direct ancestry effects to regular coreference.

For pronominal anaphora, data is less sparse, but a negative baseline (always say 0) for testing whether any pair of EDUs has a direct anaphoric link still scores over 98% accuracy. We therefore again focus on the distribution of cases exhibiting some anaphoric links in Figure 6.

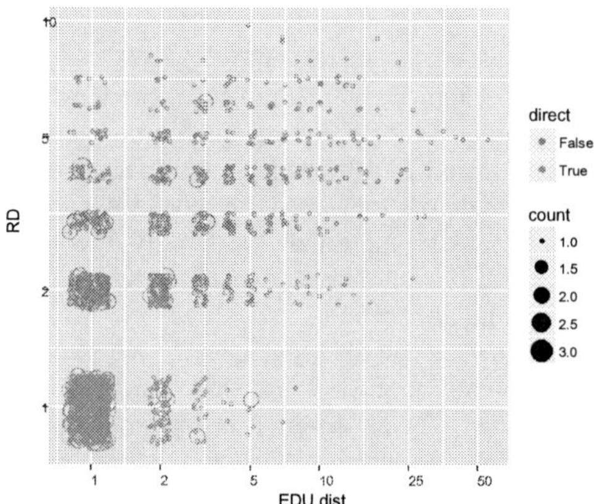

Figure 6. RD versus EDU distance for anaphora.

The picture is similar to bridging, but more dense, with 40.5% of pairs/42.5% of cases having $ED=RD=1$. Somewhat higher RD values are seen even at close EDU proximity, suggesting surface proximity is more influential for anaphora, and close RD is more critical to bridging.

4.3 Predicting coreference density

So far we have only considered unlabeled RST distance, without looking at specific RST relations or properties of the underlying units other than length. Although the DEH does not presuppose any expectations for these factors directly, it is interesting to consider which RST relations and what kinds of EDUs play into the DEH, and which are less in line with the hypothesis. To test this, we first examine which RST relations are more likely to exhibit coreference between head and dependent.

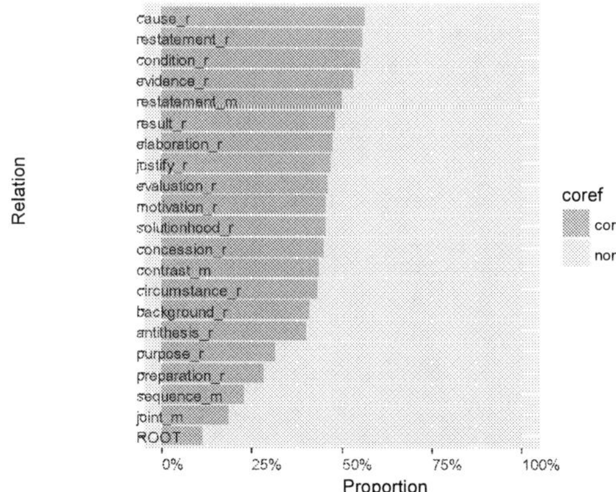

Figure 7. Proportion of EDUs showing coreference with their dependency heads by relation.

Figure 7 shows a rather broad variation in proportion of coreferentiality by relation, especially in the bottom 5 relation types (from *Purpose* down). *Cause* and *Restatement* are unsurprisingly at the top, while typically coordinating multinuclear relations such as *Sequence* and *Joint* are at the bottom. These results suggest that relation type may be a relevant predictor modulating domain or path effects on coreference likelihood.[4]

Given everything we've seen above, it seems likely that we can create a multifactorial model to predict how likely an EDU is to contain the antecedent of a given mention, which could outperform a binary 'accessible/inaccessible' DRA definition. To test this, we generate a randomized test set of 10% of EDU pairs (~17K) in the data, stratified by coreference prevalence (same proportions of single coreferent mention, 2, 3, 4… as in the rest of the data). Using the Python implementation in sklearn, we train an Extra Trees Random Forest regressor (Geurts et al. 2006%GeurtsErnstWehenkel2006) on the features outlined in Section 3.2 to predict exact coreference degree (number of coreferent mentions) and a classifier for the presence of coreference (yes/no). We also train baseline classifiers (clf) and regressors (reg) on RD and EDU distance only. Table 1 shows the results.

features	RMSE (reg)	accuracy (clf)
EDU	95.01	78.36
RD	94.53	78.79
all	**71.07**	**86.83**

Table 1. Classification accuracy for binary coreferentiality and root mean square error for regression on exact mention pair count for unseen EDU pairs.

The regressor with all features achieves a root-mean-square error of 71%, meaning it is usually about 0.71 mentions away from the true coreferent mention count. Using only EDU distance or RD is worse, at about 0.95 RMSE (Root Mean Square Error). For classification of binary coreferentiality, using all features gives a gain of ~8% accuracy, close to 87% vs. close to 79% for RD and closer to 78% for EDU distance. Classifier feature importances based on Gini indices are shown in Figure 8.

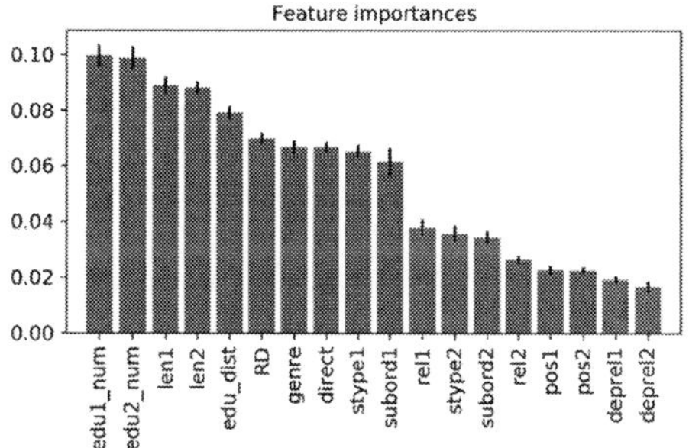

Figure 8. Variable importances for the binary classifier. Error bars give standard deviations for each feature.

The most relevant predictors, before examining any distance metrics, are the positions of the two EDUs (EDU1 is the earlier, antecedent EDU) and their lengths. This is not surprising, since late EDUs in a text have a chance to refer to more mentions, and long EDUs have more mentions. These predictors are not relevant to the DRA framework, but they are important confounds that have gone largely ignored to date. Immediately following, we see the two distance measures, with EDU distance slightly ahead of RD, and genre (another critical confound) and direct ancestry next. The remaining variables give more information about the function of the specific EDUs, including RST relations (cf. Figure 7), utterance types, clause subordination information and grammatical functions. All of these have some influence on coreference likelihood (see e.g. Trnavac & Taboada

---

[4] For *Purpose*, a partial reason may be that the frequent infinitive '… (in order) to do X' suppresses the unexpressed infinitive subject (i.e. the 'doer' is not expressed and cannot be pronominalized). I thank Paul Portner for this suggestion.

2012%TrnavacTaboada2012 on the importance of subordination for cataphora).

5 Discussion

The results of the models in the previous section, as well as individual correlations with predictors shown in Figures 4-7 demonstrate that a binary model of accessibility in DRAs is unnecessarily impoverished. We can get much better prediction accuracy for coreference domains using a multifactorial model, which is also intuitively plausible: sentence length and position are expected to have an influence, and not all RST relations and sentence types are equal with respect to coreference likelihood. The results also support the conclusion that RD and EDU distance metrics are both useful, and can be used in conjunction.

It is important to note that the features examined in this paper are EDU based, and RST graph-based, since our focus has been on properties that make a pair of EDUs likely to form a domain of coreference. It goes without saying that actual prediction of coreferentiality should take into account the inventory and properties of referring expressions within those EDUs. Thus although the classifier above is far from being able to predict exact coreference density using our features, its prediction accuracy may be considered surprisingly good considering the fact that it knows nothing about the entity types, agreement class compatibility, or even count of nominal expressions in each EDU. Although this remains outside of the scope of this paper, it seems likely that this type of information can be integrated in approaches using RST based features for prior coreference likelihood, together with established coreference resolution features.

References

Nicholas Asher. 1993. *Reference to Abstract Objects in Discourse*. Dordrecht: Kluwer.

Nicholas Asher and Alex Lascarides. 1998. Bridging. *Journal of Semantics* 15(1):83–113.

Nicholas Asher and Alex Lascarides. 2003. *Logics of Conversation*. (Studies in Natural Language Processing.) Cambridge: Cambridge University Press.

R. Harald Baayen. 2008. *Analyzing Linguistic Data. A Practical Introduction to Statistics using R*. Cambridge: Cambridge University Press.

Chloe Braud, Barbara Plank and Anders Søgaard. 2016. Multi-View and Multi-Task Training of RST Dis-course Parsers. In *Proceedings of COLING 2016*. Osaka, 1903–1913.

Lynn Carlson, Daniel Marcu and Mary Ellen Okurowski. 2001. Building a Discourse-Tagged Corpus in the Framework of Rhetorical Structure Theory. In *Proceedings of 2nd SIGDIAL Workshop on Discourse and Dialogue, Eurospeech 2001*. Aalborg, 1–10.

Christian Chiarcos and Olga Krasavina. 2008. Rhetorical Distance Revisited: A Parametrized Approach. In Anton Benz and Peter Kühnlein (eds.), *Constraints in Discourse*. Amsterdam and Philadelphia: John Benjamins, 97–115.

Kevin Clark and Christopher D. Manning. 2015. Entity-Centric Coreference Resolution with Model Stacking. In *Proceedings of ACL-IJCNLP 2015*. Beijing, 1405–1415.

Dan Cristea, Nancy Ide, Daniel Marcu and Valentin Tablan. 1999. Discourse Structure and Co-Reference: An Empirical Study. In *Proceedings of the Workshop on the Relationship Between Discourse/Dialogue Structure and Reference*. College Park, MD, 46–53.

Dan Cristea, Nancy Ide and Laurent Romary. 1998. Veins Theory: A Model of Global Discourse Cohesion and Coherence. In *Proceedings of ACL/COLING*. Montreal, Canada, 281–285.

Greg Durrett, Taylor Berg-Kirkpatrick and Dan Klein. 2016. Learning-Based Single-Document Summarization with Compression and Anaphoricity Constraints. In *Proceedings of ACL 2016*. Berlin, 1998–2008.

Greg Durrett and Dan Klein. 2014. A Joint Model for Entity Analysis: Coreference, Typing, and Linking. *Transactions of the ACL* 2:477–490.

Pierre Geurts, Damien Ernst and Louis Wehenkel. 2006. Extremely Randomized Trees. *Machine Learning* 63(1):3–42.

Katsuhiko Hayashi, Tsutomu Hirao and Masaaki Nagata. 2016. Empirical Comparison of Dependency Conversions for RST Discourse Trees. In *SIGDIAL 2016*. Los Angeles, 128–136.

Tsutomu Hirao, Yasuhisa Yoshida, Masaaki Nishino, Norihito Yasuda and Masaaki Nagata. 2013. Single-Document Summarization as a Tree Knapsack Problem. In *EMNLP 2013*. Seattle, 1515–1520.

Eduard Hovy, Mitchell Marcus, Martha Palmer, Lance Ramshaw and Ralph Weischedel. 2006. OntoNotes: The 90% Solution. In *Proceedings of the Human Language Technology Conference of the NAACL, Companion Volume: Short Papers*. New York, 57–60.

Ryu Iida and Takenobu Tokunaga. 2012. A Metric for Evaluating Discourse Coherence based on Coreference Resolution. In *Proceedings of COLING 2012*. Mumbai, 483–494.

Rhetorical relation markers in Russian RST Treebank

Svetlana Toldova (1), Dina Pisarevskaya (2), Margarita Ananyeva (3),
Maria Kobozeva (3), Alexander Nasedkin (1), Sofia Nikiforova (1),
Irina Pavlova (1), and Alexey Shelepov (1)
1 NRU Higher School of Economics, Moscow, Russia
2 Institute for Oriental Studies of the RAS, Moscow, Russia
3 Institute for Systems Analysis FRC CSC RAS
toldova@yandex.ru, dinabpr@gmail.com, ananyeva@isa.ru,
kobozeva@isa.ru, kloudsnuff@gmail.com, son.nik@mail.ru,
ispavlovais@gmail.com, alexshelepov1992@gmail.com

Abstract

The paper deals with the pilot version of the first RST discourse treebank for Russian. The project started in 2016. At present, the treebank consists of sixty news texts annotated for rhetorical relations according to RST scheme. However, this scheme was slightly modified in order to achieve higher inter-annotator agreement score. During the annotation procedure, we also registered the discourse connectives of different types and mapped them onto the corresponding rhetoric relations. In present paper, we discuss our experience of RST scheme adaptation for Russian news texts. Besides, we report on the distribution of the most frequent discourse connectives in our corpus.

1 Introduction

One of the focuses of the present NLP research is the text analysis on the discourse level. There is a big amount of NLP tasks, such as coreference resolution, text summarization, irony detection, question-answering systems etc., where the analysis of text needs to go beyond the boundaries of a single clause or even a sentence. For such tasks, the information on text cohesion, discourse structure and discourse relations is needed. In order to develop the modules dealing with discourse analysis, one needs a text corpus with discourse level annotation.

This paper describes the creation of the pilot version of the Discourse-annotated corpus for the Russian language, based on Rhetorical Structure Theory (RST) framework (Mann, Thompson, 1988). Corpus includes the texts taken from Russian freely available online resources and manually annotated for RST relations. It is designed for conducting the experiments on different machine-learning methods for discourse parsing. It also can be used for the investigation of discourse structure, relational and lexical cohesion and other discourse-based phenomena in Russian.

During the annotation procedure we single out different connectives (conjunctions, particles, some lexical and punctuation cues), associated with the corresponding discourse relation. These cues can serve as a seed set for automatic discourse connectives extraction.

Until now, the majority of theoretical works devoted to discourse relation for Russian were dealing primarily with the analysis of conjunction, parenthesis words and expressions functions. Our approach differs in that our goal was to find out what lexical items irrespective of their part of speech can signal the presence of a rhetorical relation. Thus, we take into consideration such lexical clues as nouns or verbs of speech etc. (e.g. *prichina* 'the

29

Proceedings of the 6th Workshop Recent Advances in RST and Related Formalisms, pages 29–33,
Santiago de Compostela, Spain, September 4 2017. ©2017 Association for Computational Linguistics

course'). In present paper, we suggest quantitative analyses of these connectives.

2 Related works

There exist different approaches to discourse annotation principles. One of the approaches is based on the "linear" annotation. Thus, in Penn Discourse Treebank (PDTB) discourse relations are lexically anchored by discourse connectives. They are viewed as predicates that take abstract objects such as propositions, events and states as their arguments (PDTB (Prasad et al., 2007; Webber et al., 2016), TurkishDB (Zeyrek et al., 2013), etc.). In the Chinese Discourse TreeBank the punctuation marks also play role in the annotation (Zhou, Xue, 2015). Models based on cohesive relations are not tree-like, for instance, Discourse Graphbank (Wolf and Gibson, 2005). Another significant approach is the Rhetorical Structure Theory (RST) (Mann, Thompson, 1988). RST framework represents text as a hierarchy of elementary discourse units (EDUs) and describes relations between them and between bigger parts of text. Some EDUs carry more important information (nucleus) than others (satellite) do. There are two rhetorical relation types: nucleus-satellite (mononuclear) and multi-nuclear. While the first type connects a nucleus and a satellite, the latter includes EDUs that are equally important in the analyzed discourse. For the current research we chose RST to study cohesive markers and discourse cues taking into consideration 'trees' - discourse structure of texts.

There exist special lexicons or extensive descriptions of discourse connectives' (their types, positions, linking directions, ambiguous degrees, distribution of signalled relations) for particular languages: e.g. for English (Taboada M., Das D, 2013), for French (Roze C., Danlos L., Muller P. LEXCONN), for Chinese (Huang H. H. et al., 2014), etc. There are also comparatives studies of discourse connectives (e.g. English and French (Popescu-Belis A. et al, 2012), Spanish and Chinese (Cao S., da Cunha I., Bel N, 2016)).

As some discourse markers can indicate more than one discourse relation, another problem in this field is a lexical cue disambiguation (da Cunha I., 2013; Khazaei T. et al., 2015). General way of resolving this problem is extracting syntactic contexts for a particular cue in different discourse relation.

For automatic discourse parsing the most complicated task is to identify implicit discourse relations - those that do not involve any explicit discourse connectives. In (Rutherford A. et al., 2015) authors investigated the criteria for selecting the discourse connectives that can be omitted without changing the context.

M. Taboada and D. Das (Taboada M., Das D, 2013) suggest an exhaustive investigation of discourse relation clues. Besides traditionally discussed functional words, such as conjunctions, the list of connectives features is extended by means of semantic, syntactic, graphical and others types of features. As a result, authors show that the majority of relations are explicit rather than implicit, as it is usually postulated. Making a list of discourse relations clues for Russian, we take this approach into consideration.

3 Russian RST Bank

The current project started in 2016. We are planning to annotate texts (more than 100,000 tokens) of four genres and domains: science, popular science, news stories, and analytic journalism. The pilot project was aimed at working-out annotation rules and to achieve a reasonable score for inter-annotator agreement.

For annotation we use an open-source tool rstWeb [https://corpling.uis.georgetown.edu/rst-web/info/]. It has a number of advantages in comparison with other tools (UAM CorpusTool, RSTTool, GraphAnno): user-friendly interface, ability to work in the browser and to make changes to the code.

We start with the list of relations suggested in (Mann W., Tompson S., 1988). The instruction for annotators was based on the work by L.Carlson, D. Marcu, M. Okurowsky (Carlson et al., 2003). However, the initial list of relations was slightly modified. After modification, the resulting list consisted of 25 relations. During the further tagging procedure, special focus was on inter-annotator agreement (IAA). We have selected Krippendorff's unitized alpha as a statistic to measure IAA. It operates on the whole annotation spans instead of isolated tokens and it can be calculated for any number of annotators.

It turned out that annotators confuse Volitional and Non-Volitional relations, Antithesis and Contrast (same meaning, but Antithesis is mononuclear, Contrast - multinuclear), Cause and Effect (same meaning, but either cause or effect is nuclear). We decided to tack them, as well as two types of Attribution (a general and more specific one) and Interpretation with Evaluation (the only difference is in the degree of objectivity of author's evaluation). Besides, we took out Conclusion and Motivation, since they occur rarely and the first one can be considered a subtype of Restatement). Finally, we got 17 relations that were divided into four groups (fig. 1). These modifications have given a vast improvement of IAA. For three texts tagged by four people it stood at 0,27 - 0,49 before reduction of the relations tree and 0,69 - 0,77 after reduction. In order to accelerate the annotation process, the automatic text segmentation was

1. Coherence
    1.1. Background
    1.2. Elaboration
    1.3. Restatement
    1.4. Interpretation - Evaluation
    1.5. Preparation
    1.6. Solutionhood
2. Casual-argumentative
    2.1. Contrastive
        2.1.1. Concession
        2.1.2. Contrast
    2.2. Causal
        2.2.1. Purpose
        2.2.2. Evidence
        2.2.3. Cause-Effect
    2.3. Condition
3. Structural
    3.1. Sequence
    3.2. Joint
    3.3. Same-unit
    3.4. Comparison
4. Attribution
    4.1. Attribution

Figure 1. The list of rhetoric relations

applied. RusClaSp (http://gree-gorey.github.io/) package was taken as a basis and adapted to our task and corpus. In particular, we consider some explicit unambiguous markers and ignore parenthetic phrases. The human-annotator checks the result of automatic segmentation and builds a discourse tree of a text.

By now, we have annotated 73 texts, mostly news stories (each of them is 30 sentences in length on the average), they contain 44685 tokens. For each text we built one single tree where text spans are connected to other spans, nodes are connected to other nodes, and so on to the common vertex.

4   Rhetorical relations markers

In our current research, we investigate the interaction between discourse connectives and the discourse relations. As it has been already mentioned, we consider not only functional words to be rhetoric relation markers. The markers includes punctuation marks, prepositions, pronouns, speech verbs, etc.

While annotating the corpus, we register overt clues for corresponding relation types. The list of registered cases consists of 692 pairs "marker-relation" (with approximately 200-250 unique markers suggested by annotators). The variation in number of markers due to the fact that some the markers are constructions where one of their elements may vary. For instance, one of the patterns for ATTRIBUTION relation is a construction introducing "reported speech" consisting of a verb of speech plus, optionally, a conjunction *chto* 'what, that' (e.g. "said that" or "reported that" etc.). There is no enough data to decide whether to treat the elements of this construction as separate markers or not.

Markers, which appear in texts more frequently, may be ambiguous, i.e. same markers can signal several relations. There are 55 markers ordered by the raise of their frequencies (threshold >= 3 occurrences in the corpus) in fig. 2.

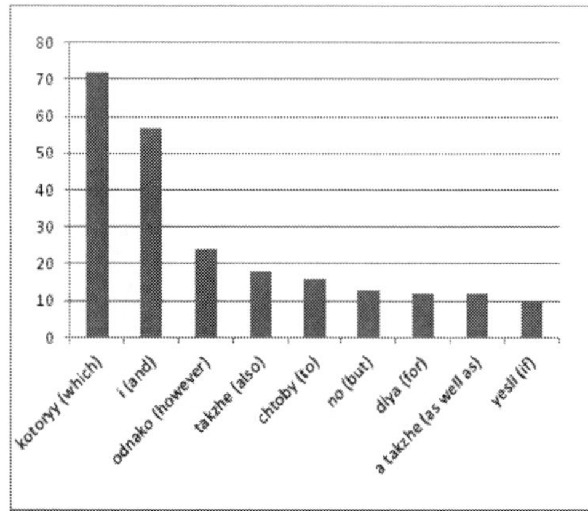
Figure 2. The frequency of top 55 markers

Among 14 most frequent markers (threshold >=9), most of them (with one exception of *v to vremya,, kak* 'at time, when') point directly on the definite relation type or close relation types. The table 1 presents the statistics for relations expressed overtly via markers. The most frequent marker for this relation is given.

Relation type	Freq	marker	translation
Elaboration	150	*kotoryj*	"which, that"
Joint	119	*i, takzhe*	and, as well
Attribution	118	*zajavil, soobschil*	report, announce etc.
Contrast	62	*Odnako, a, no*	However, but
Cause-Effect	47	*Poetomu, V+prichina*	so, accordingly, V+*cause*
Purpose	39	*Chtoby, dlya*	In order that, for
Interpretation-Evaluation	34	Nouns and verbs expressing opinion	
Background	31	No dominant marker	
Condition	27	*esli*	if

Table 1. Relations with their most frequent markers

As we can see from the table the most frequent relation in News texts are ELABORATION, JOINT and ATTRIBUTION. These texts are characterized by high proportion of symmetric relations and high quantity of special lexical expressions such as constructions with speech verbs and other types of mental predicates.

5 Discussion

The discourse markers analysis reveals some interesting evidence that deserves additional attention. Firstly, the news texts contain not many special subordinate conjunctions for reason, cause etc. The most frequent are such relations as JOINT, ELABORATION and ATTRIBUTION.

The punctuation marks in Russian such as hyphen can also signal some relations, namely, ELABORATION.

The JOINT relation is expressed not only via coordinative conjunction, but also via the conjunction *a* "but" traditionally treated as adversative.

The clause type for elaboration in Russian news texts is a relative clause (finite clause or participial clause). Thus, the marker for elaboration is the relative pronoun *kotoryj* 'which'.

The task to extract the ATTRIBUTION relation can be reformulated as the task to extract the markers of reported speech. Almost all the markers that the annotators single out for ATTRIBUTION are special constructions for reported speech introduction into discourse such as 'said that', 'according to X's opinion', 'As X's announced…'

There is a tendency in News texts to express cause-effect and some other relations via special lexemes denoting some mental operations (assessment, intentions etc.).

6 Conclusions

The aim of this paper was to introduce an ongoing project on a new RST TreeBank construction and to discuss our experience of adopting the RST scheme for rhetoric relations annotation for Russian. We also have provided a pilot research of different types of discourse clues. We are going to use some of these clues as a seed set for bootstrapping some other discourse markers and map them for specific rhetoric relations. The survey of different markers extracted by the annotators is helpful for feature extraction for developing a discourse parser for Russian based on machine learning.

Acknowledgements

This research was supported by a grant from Russian Foundation for Basic Research Fund (15-07-09306).

References

A. Popescu-Belis, T. Meyer, J. Liyanapathirana, B.Cartoni, and Zufferey S. 2012. Discourse-level annotation over Europarl for machine translation: Connectives and pronouns. *In Proceedings of the eighth international conference on Language Resources and Evaluation (LREC)*. № EPFL-CONF-192582: 2716-2720.

A. Rutherford and N. Xue. 2015. Improving the Inference of Implicit Discourse Relations via Classifying Explicit Discourse Connectives. *HLT-NAACL*: 799-808.

Bonnie Webber, Rashmi Prasad, Alan Lee, and Aravind Joshi. 2016. A Discourse-Annotated Corpus of Conjoined VPs. *Proc. 10th Linguistics Annotation Workshop*, Berlin: 22–31.

C. Roze, L. Danlos, and P. Muller. 2012. LEXCONN: a French lexicon of discourse connectives. In Discours. Revue de linguistique, psycholinguistique et informatique. *A journal of linguistics, psycholinguistics and computational linguistics*. №. 10.

D. Zeyrek, I. Demirşahin, A.B. Sevdik Çallı, and R. Çakıcı. 2013. Turkish Discourse Bank: Porting a discourse annotation style to a morphologically rich language. *Dialogue and Discourse, 4(2)*: 174–184.

Florian Wolf and Edward Gibson. 2005. Representing discourse coherence: *A corpus-based study. In Computational Linguistics, 31(2)*: 249–287.

H.-H. Huang, T.-W. Chang, H.-E. Chen, and H.-H. Chen. 2014. Interpretation of Chinese Discourse Connectives for Explicit Discourse Relation Recognition. *Proceedings of COLING* 2014: 632-643.

Iria da Cunha, Juan-Manuel Torres-Moreno, and Gerardo Sierra. 2011. On the development of the RST Spanish treebank. *Proceedings of the 5th Linguistic Annotation Workshop (LAW V)*. 1–10.

L. Carlson, D. Marcu, M.E. Okurowski. 2003. Building a Discourse-Tagged Corpus in the Framework of Rhetorical Structure Theory, Current directions in discourse and dialogue, Kluwer Academic Publishers: 85–112.

M. Taboada. 2013. Das D. Annotation upon Annotation: Adding Signalling Information to a Corpus of Discourse Relations. In D&D. Vol.. 4. №. 2: 249-281.

N. van der Vliet, I. Berzlanovich, G. Bouma, M. Egg, and G. Redeker. 2011. Building a Discourse-Annotated Dutch Text Corpus. *Proceedings of the Workshop "Beyond Semantics: Corpus-based Investigations of Pragmatic and Discourse Phenomena"*, Goettingen, Germany, 23–25 February 2011: 157–171.

Rashmi Prasad, Eleni Miltsakaki, Nikhil Dinesh, Alan Lee, Aravind Joshi, Livio Robaldo, and Bonnie Webber. 2007. The Penn Discourse Treebank 2.0 Annotation Manual. Technical Report 203, Institute for Research in Cognitive Science, University of Pennsylvania.

Rashmi Prasad, Nikhil Dinesh, Alan Lee, Eleni Miltsakaki, Livio Robaldo, Aravind Joshi, and Bonnie Webber. 2008. The Penn discourse treebank 2.0. *Proceedings of the 6th International Conference on Language Resources and Evaluation*: 2961–2968.

S. Cao, I. da Cunha, and N. Bel. 2016. An analysis of the Concession relation based on the discourse marker aunque in a Spanish-Chinese parallel corpus. *Procesamiento del Lenguaje Natural*. Vol. 56: 81-88.

S. Joty, G. Carenini, and R. T. Ng. 2015. CODRA: A Novel Discriminative Framework for Rhetorical Analysis. In Computational Linguistics 41, 3: 385-435.

S.Y. Cao, I. da Cunha, and M. Iruskieta. 2016. Elaboration of a Spanish-Chinese parallel corpus with translation and language learning purposes, *34th International Conference of the Spanish Society for Applied Linguistics (AESLA)*, to appear.

I. da Cunha. 2013. A Symbolic Corpus-based Approach to Detect and Solve the Ambiguity of Discourse Markers, *Research in Computing Science* 70: 93-104.

T. Khazaei, L. Xiao, and R.E. Mercer. 2015. Identification and Disambiguation of Lexical Cues of Rhetorical Relations across Different Text Genres. Workshop on Linking Models of Lexical, Sentential and Discourse-level Semantics (LSDSem): 54 63.

W.C. Mann and S.A. Thompson. 1988. Rhetorical Structure Theory: Toward a Functional Theory of Text Organization, *Text 8*, 3, 1988: 243–281.

Y. Zhou and N. Xue. 2015. The Chinese Discourse TreeBank: A Chinese corpus annotated with discourse relations. *Language Resources and Evaluation*: 397–431.

Applying the Rhetorical Structure Theory in Alzheimer patients' speech [*]

Anayeli Paulino and **Gerardo Sierra**
Grupo de Ingeniería Lingüística
Instituto de Ingeniería
Universidad Nacional Autónoma de México
ApaulinoJ@iingen.unam.mx
GSierraM@iingen.unam.mx

Abstract

In the present paper, semi-structured interviews conducted on 7 Spanish speaking Alzheimer-type Dementia patients and on 6 Spanish speaking adults with healthy aging processes are examined. Rhetorical Structure Theory was used to analyze each of the turns. The procedure involves the segmentation of Semantic Dialog Units (SDU´s), rhetorical relations labeling and the construction of tree diagrams. Preliminary results indicate a marked difference in number of rhetoric relations used by both our samples, in which the relations of elaboration, concession, justify and restatement are the most frequently used by Alzheimer-type dementia patients.

1 Introduction

Dementia of Alzheimer´s type (DAT) is a neurodegenerative disease in which at least three cognitive spheres are affected: memory, agnosia and visuospatial skills and language; hitherto, the only definite diagnosis can be determined posmortem.

While linguistic deficits in each phase of dementia have been studied for decades with the intention of identifying the linguistic phenomena which can be significant for a possible diagnosis (Appell, 1982; Kemper, 1991; Emery, 2001), never until recent years has proposal in the field of Natural Language Processing (NLP) been dedicated to utilizing the most frequent and useful linguistic deficits, so that, with the help of computational analysis, viable tools in identifying the disease at an early stage can be created.

Thus, recent studies using automated or semiautomated identification have relied on different linguistic criteria such a lexical clues (Bucks et al., 2010; Asgari, Kaye and Dogde, 2017), syntactic complexity (Roark, Mitchel and Hollingshead, 2007), discourse phenomena (Habash, 2011) and even prosodic elements found in narrative language samples (Köning, et al., 2015).

Despite these efforts, there are still limitations as the vast majority of researches have focused solely on English speaking populations. One of the challenges researches have dealt with is using a multiethnic-large- scale Corpus for their studies. Currently Hernández and Ratté (2016) in collaboration with the Carolinas Conversation Collection (Pope and Davis, 2011) are seeking to compile a multiethnic English-Spanish Corpus with the objective to develope an automated tool to detect the most common linguistic deficits in dementia patients.

As an alternative for an innovative analysis that be at the same time useful in the automatic identification of DAT, this paper is based on the Carolinas Conversations Corpus in Spanish and it presents the methodology and first findings on a discourse analysis conducted on Dementia of Alzheimer-type patients using the Rhetorical Structure Theory, RST (Mann and Thompson, 1988). Specifically, the method followed was taken from Maite Taboada´s study (2004). The purpose is to identify and extract patterns in the discourse relations (also known

---

[*]This work is supported by CONACYT under the project *Ampliación del corpus multiétnico de conversaciones con personas de edad avanzada* in collaboration with the Grupo de Ingeniería Lingüística, UNAM, the École de Technologie Supérieure, Montréal and the Universidad Técnica Particular de Loja, Ecuador.

Proceedings of the 6th Workshop Recent Advances in RST and Related Formalisms, pages 34–38,
Santiago de Compostela, Spain, September 4 2017. ©2017 Association for Computational Linguistics

as rhetorical relations) both in the conversations of Alzheimer-type Dementia patients and normal elderly adults.

2 Related Work

Since its proposal, RST has been envisioned as a theoretical model of much utility in the field of Natural Language Processing; evidence of this are the multiple applications in areas as diverse as automatic text summaries, automatic translation, parallel corpus, subjective content analysis and textual similarity among many others.

2.1 RST for Analysis of Conversations

The study of spoken discourse has also been the focus of attention of the inquiries concerning RST. Within this field we find the studies by Fawcet and Davies (1992) who propose an analysis of monologue, which can serve as an autonomous discourse unit. Using the original RST proposal by Mann and Thompson, Amanda Stent (2000) offers a new method for segmentation and relations to perform an analysis through turns form which new concepts of relations were created. Moreover, prosodic elements are integrated so as to perform the segmentation.

Maite Taboada (2004) proposes a dialogic analysis method adhering to the original RST. She analyses conversations in Spanish and English from JANUS corpus. Her analysis is contrastive and qualitative intra and inter turns. In her results, she demonstrates that a dialogic analysis can be performed on any language; in addition, she proves that RST is a reliable method to be implemented in spoken discourse.

Other proposals which are not as closely related to RST and which integrate other phenomena have been suggested: DAMSL (Core and Allen, 1997) uses a three layer scheme which integrates the actions of speech along with other filters such as the communicative functions and utterances features. On the other hand, ISO (Bunt et al., 2010) integrates the acts of speech and the classification of emotions for their application in the analysis of dialogs.

2.2 RST in the Analysis of Dementia

Up to this point, no study which retakes RST for the discourse analysis on dementia patients has been encountered yet. This notes that whilst RST has had a wide application in areas of computational linguistics, it has not yet been implemented in other interdisciplinary fields such as clinical linguistics.

Notwithstanding this, in the treatment of linguistics deficits, interesting proposals have started to be formulated such as Kong et al. (2017). They used RST in narrations and descriptions of aphasia patients and healthy adults. In the report, it is pointed out that the affected patients produce less discourse units. A breakthrough in this analysis is that the study was strictly discourse-based contrasting the majority of other studies which are based on lexical analysis alone.

3 Method

In this section the procedure of this study is described. The criterion for transcription, the labeling of rhetoric relations and the construction and analysis of discourse trees were applied both in injured patients and caregivers. As it was commented before, for the theoretical framework, the analysis proposed by Taboada (2004) was reconsidered for the following reasons: firstly, the author's proposal is the one which most adheres to the standard structure of RST which has the support of a variety of studies; secondly, one of the corpora used was in Spanish, as a consequence the author discusses and takes into account some of the phenomena which are typical of Spanish at the moment of her analysis.

3.1 Corpus

In this study, the Carolinas Conversation Corpus in Spanish, which integrates semi-structured interviews conducted on elder adults with Alzheimer disease, elder adults in a healthy aging process, and elder adults with other neurodegenerative diseases was used. The sample consisted of 7 adults diagnosed with Dementia of Alzheimer type in mild and moderate stages (6 women, 1 man; average age: 84.57), and 6 healthy elderly control participants (6 women; average age: 84). All of the participants lived in Ecuador and were Spanish speakers. Additionally, the alias given by the Carolinas corpus were preserved to protect their privacy. The period between conversations goes from 6 to 50 minutes.

Relation	Murrieta		Cortés		San Juan		Vicario		Mora		Zamacona		Buendía	
Antithesis	2	3%	0	0%	0	0%	3	7%	0	0%	0	0%	2	4%
Concession	3	5%	0	0%	2	11%	0	0%	0	0%	2	14%	1	2%
Condition	4	7%	0	0%	0	0%	1	2%	0	0%	1	7%	0	0%
Elaboration	22	36%	0	0%	12	63%	14	31%	6	38%	3	21%	14	31%
Evaluation	2	3%	0	0%	2	11%	1	2%	0	0%	0	0%	0	0%
Evidence	6	10%	0	0%	0	0%	0	0%	0	0%	1	7%	2	4%
Justify	3	5%	0	0%	1	5%	6	13%	2	13%	0	0%	3	7%
Motivation	1	2%	1	20%	0	0%	0	0%	0	0%	0	0%	1	2%
Restatement	3	5%	1	20%	0	0%	3	7%	4	25%	2	14%	2	4%
V Cause	3	5%	0	0%	1	5%	2	4%	0	0%	0	0%	1	2%
V Result	0	0%	1	20%	0	0%	2	4%	0	0%	0	0%	3	7%

Table 1: Most frequent Presentational and Subject Matter Relations formulated by DAT patients

3.2 Annotation criteria

The norms of the Carolinas Conversations corpus were used. The procedure involved separation in turns (caregiver-patient), followed by the transcription at an orthographic level. For the orthographic level, the conventional signs for punctuation were used: periods, commas, quotation marks, question and exclamation marks. With regards to the prosodic level, intonation phenomena were included (rising/falling), pitch of the voice and long and short pauses (starting from a second on). Finally, in form of comments, kinesthetic phenomena were noted (gestures, sighs, movements), as well as noises and idiolect phenomena for each participant (for instance, use of contractions and diminutives).

For the transcription, the computer program Transcriber 1.5.1 (Boudahmane et al., 2008) was used; the files were converted into txt format so that they could be handled better.

3.3 Segmentation criteria

In the initial RST proposal, the minimum units are defined as EDU´s (Elementary Discourse Units); they refer to clauses which express a complete meaning (Mann and Thompson, 1988: 6). From this, it is deduced that the segmentation criteria relies on semantic and syntactic limits.

The segmentation units in this study were adapted to the characteristics of the conversational analysis and were denominated as SDU´s (Semantic Dialogue Units) (Maite Taboada, 2004: 44). Basically, SDU´s are utterances delimited by prosodic features (intonation, pauses), syntactic forms (presence of conjugated verb forms, complements and discourse markers) and semantic criteria (semantic completeness). Semantic units can be compared to previously coined concepts in the field of discourse as "information units" (Halliday, 1967) or "intonation units" (Chafe, 1994). These segmentation criteria are also considered in the analysis by Kong et al. (2017).

An important aspect to keep in mind during the segmentation is the quantity of anomalies presented by patients.The reformulations, the incomplete statements and the unusually long pauses were relatively frequent, therefore, there were some concessions made. For example, syntactic criteria were established as a more reliable limit; however, if there were confusions, the pitch or the intonation disambiguated the boundaries between units. Similarly, on multiple occasions the patient was unable to complete a semantic unit. For these cases, a statement was considered a SDU if it included a conjugated verb and if it was relatively understandable.

3.4 Labelling

The rhetoric relations, also known as a coherence or discourse relations (Taboada and Mann, 2006), connect each SDU through functional and semantic features (Mann and Thompson: 5) and the criterion of nuclearity between two semantic units.

During the labeling, it was decided to adhere to the standard classification due to the fact that it is one of the most commonly used classifications; furthermore, unlike others, the number of relations does not hinder identification. The classification was taken form the official RST web-page.[1]

---

[1] `www.sfu.ca/rst/`

Relation	Zubarán		DelCarpio		Remedios		Luna		Allende		Restrepo	
Antithesis	6	5%	2	2%	0	0%	1	3%	3	5%	3	3%
Background	2	2%	4	5%	4	3%	1	3%	2	4%	3	3%
Concession	9	8%	2	2%	4	3%	5	16%	5	9%	6	6%
Elaboration	30	27%	30	35%	55	40%	10	32%	18	32%	15	16%
Evaluation	2	2%	2	2%	1	1%	0	0%	3	5%	8	8%
Evidence	16	15%	12	14%	6	4%	1	3%	2	4%	1	1%
Interpretation	3	3%	2	2%	1	1%	0	0%	1	2%	2	2%
Justify	3	3%	4	5%	10	7%	2	6%	1	2%	7	7%
N-V Result	3	3%	0	0%	1	1%	0	0%	4	7%	5	5%
Restatement	8	7%	3	3%	4	3%	0	0%	1	2%	18	19%
Summary	5	5%	4	5%	3	2%	0	0%	0	0%	1	1%
V Cause	0	0%	5	6%	6	4%	0	0%	2	4%	3	3%
V Result	2	2%	8	9%	7	5%	2	6%	1	2%	4	4%

Table 2: Most frequent Presentational and Subject Matter Relations formulated by healthy elderly controls

3.5 Discursive-trees elaboration

For the building of discursive-trees, the RSTTool program (O´ Donell, 2004) was employed. Besides the diagrams, this tool offers a statistical section in which it counts the total EDU´s and the number of rhetorical relations used in the conversations.

In this first phase it was only applied an intra-turn analysis. The elaboration of discourse trees follows one of the fundamental principles of the theory: the principle of hierarchy between spans and relation schemas (Taboada and Mann, 2006). According to Taboada (2004), the making of discourse trees implies studying the entire text (in this case the entire turn of the patient), locating the biggest, most important and general segments from the surface, and disintegrating them into smaller units. A second analysis is performed inversely: from small units to general ones. In this work both process were made.

Taking into account that an interlocutor always tries to take advantages of their interventions, a nuclear SDU per se was not enough in some cases. It was decided to consider more nuclear semantic units inside the turn if it was required.

During this stage of analysis, anomalies in discourse were reencountered; on some occasions, mostly in the turn of dementia patients, there were ruptures which cannot be related to the main frame, among which, the segment was not united to the main structure and both were considered two different trees. Afterwards, in the organization of relations, if the segments were re- related one another, then these were united to the principal tree.

3.6 Preliminary results

Tables 1 and 2 show most frequent rhetorical relations used by DAT patients and healthy elderly controls, respectively. Until now, the results of the quantitative analysis point out that there are marked differences in the frequency of rhetoric relations produced between the population with dementia and the healthy older controls. Additionally, patients with dementia use less variety of rhetoric relations in their conversational discourse than adults without cerebral damage.

Out of all the rhetorical relations, there is a frequent use of elaboration relation in both populations. Despite the fact that the use of elaboration is more frequent that other forms of relations, particularly in the patients with Alzheimer-type dementia, other relations are recurrent as well; there are concession, justify and restatement. It is particularly remarkable that relations like enablement, unconditional and purpose were not employed by either of the groups.

Based on data, it is observed that, roughly, most used relations in elderly adults were also frequently used by DAT patients, hence, it seems that the main difference between the samples relies on the proportion of relations used.

3.7 Future Work

Even though this study employed a limited number of DAT patients, the sample allows the exploration of RST as a reliable method for describing coherence relations established between semantic units in a dialog. However, it is still necessary to carry out contrastive studies with other corpus in order to corroborate the results obtained in this work.

Many tasks are yet to be done in the present proposal, one of which is the examination of the tree diagrams of each speaker. The number of nodes and the levels of each scheme will result helpful in doing so. The analysis in between turns is still missing, which will be challenging considering the phenomena involved. Consequently, this makes them difficult to integrate into the general diagram scheme. In spite of the connection which can be established between turns, we must consider necessary restrictions that the discourse genre imposes.

This paper merely examines the discourse of a small sample of Alzheimer-type Dementia patients and healthy adults; nevertheless, the analysis method of RST seems to be viable up until its incipient stage of analysis. For this reason further applications in the field of linguistic deficits are particularly promising.

References

Alexandra Köning, Aharon Satt, Alexander Sorin, Ron Hoory, Orith T. Ronen, Alexandre Derreumaux, Valeria Manera, Franz Verhey, Pauline Aalten, Pillipe H. Robert and Renaud David. 2015. Automatic speech analysis for the assessment of patients with predementia and Alzheimer´s disease. *Alzheimer and Dementia*, 1 (1): 112-124.

Amanda Stent. 2000. Rhetorical Relations in dialog. *INLG 00 Proceedings of the first international conference on Natural Language generation*, Mitzpe, Ramón, Israel.

Antony Habash. 2012. Language analysis of speakers with dementia of the Alzheimer´s type. University of North Carolina Wilmington.

Anthony Pak-Hin Kong, Anastasia Linnik, Sam-Po Law and Waisa Wai-Man. 2017. Measuring discourse coherence in anomic aphasia using Rhetorical Structure Theory. *International Journal of Speech-Language Pathology*, 1-16.

Brian Roark, Margaret Mitchel and Kristy Hollingshead. June 2007. Syntactic complexity measure for detecting Mild Cognitive Impairment. *BioNLP 2007: Biological, translational, and clinical language processing*. Prague: 1-8.

Charlene Pope and Boyd H. Davies. 2011. Finding a balance: The Carolinas Conversation Collection. *Corpus Linguistics and Linguistic Theory*, 7(1): 143-161.

Daniel Kempler. 1991. Language Changes in Dementia of the Alzheimer Type. *Dementia and Communication*. Philadelphia, B.C. Decker.

Harry Bunt, Jan Alexandersson, Jae-Woong Choe, Alex Chengyu Fang, Koiti Hasida, Volha Petukhova, Andrei Popescu-Belis, Laurent Romary and David Traum. 2010. ISO 24617-2: A semantically-based standard for dialogue annotation. *Proceedings of LREC2012*.

Julian Appell, Andrew Kertesz and Michael Fisman. 1982. A Study of Language Functioning in Alzheimer Patients. *Brain and Language*. 17, 73-91.

Karim Boudahmane, Mathieu Manta, Fabien Antoine, Sylvain Galliano and Claude Barras. 2008. *Transcriber: a tool for segmenting, labeling and transcribing speech*.

Laura Hernández, Sylvie Ratté, Charlene Pope and Boyd H. Davis. August 11, 2016. Conversing with the elderly in Latin America: a new cohort for multimodal, multilingual longitudinal studies on aging. *Proceedings of the 7th Workshop on Cognitive Aspects of Computational Language Learning*, 16-21.

Maite Taboada. 2004. *Building coherence and cohesion: task-oriented dialogue in English and Spanish*. Amsterdam, John Benjamins.

Maite Taboada and William Mann. 2006. Rhetorical Structure Theory: looking back and moving ahead. *Discourse Studies*, 8(3): 423-459.

M.A.K. Halliday. Notes on transitivity and theme in English. *Journal of Linguistics*, 3: 177-274.

Mark G. Core and James F. Allen. 1997. Coding Dialogs with DAMSL Annotation Scheme. *AAAI fall symposium on communicative action in humans and machines*, 56.

Meysam Asgary, Jeffrey Kaye and Hiroko Dodge. 2017. Predicting mild cognitive impairment from spontaneous spoken utterances. *Alzheimer´s & Dementia*, 3: 219-228.

Mick O´Donell. 2004. *RSTTool. An RST Markup Tool*.

Olga Emery, 2001. Language impairment in dementia of the Alzheimer type: A hierarchical decline? *International Psychiatry in medicine*, 30 (2), 145-164.

Robin P. Fawcett and Bethan L. Davies. April, 1992. Monologue as a turn in dialogue: towards an integration of exchange structure and rhetorical structure theory. *6th International Workshop on Natural Language Generation*. Trente, Italy.

Wallace Chafe. 1994. *Discourse, consciousness, and time*, Chicago, The University of Chicago Press.

Willian Mann and Sandra Thompson. 1988. Rhetorical Structure Theory: Towards a functional theory of text organization. *Text*, 8, 243-281.

Using lexical level information in discourse structures for Basque sentiment analysis

Jon Alkorta
IXA research group
UPV-EHU
jon.alkorta@ehu.eus

Koldo Gojenola
IXA research group
UPV-EHU
koldo.gojenola@ehu.eus

Mikel Iruskieta
IXA research group
UPV-EHU
mikel.iruskieta@ehu.eus

Maite Taboada
Discourse Processing Lab
Simon Fraser University
mtaboada@sfu.ca

Abstract

Systems for opinion and sentiment analysis rely on different resources: a lexicon, annotated corpora and constraints (morphological, syntactic or discursive), depending on the nature of the language or text type. In this respect, Basque is a language with fewer linguistic resources and tools than other languages, like English or Spanish. The aim of this work is to study whether some kinds of discourse structures based on nuclearity are sufficient to correctly assign positive and negative polarity with a lexicon-based approach for sentiment analysis. The evaluation is performed in two phases: i) Text extraction following some constraints on discourse structure from manually annotated trees. ii) Automatic annotation of semantic orientation (or polarity). Results show that the method is useful to detect all positive cases, but fails with the negative ones. An error analysis shows that negative cases have to be addressed in a different way. The immediate results of this work include an evaluation on how discourse structure can be exploited in Basque. In the future, we will also publish a manually created Basque dictionary to use in sentiment analysis tasks.

1 Introduction

Sentiment analysis is "the field of study that analyzes people's opinions, sentiments, evaluations, appraisals, attitudes, and emotions towards entities such as products, services, organizations, individuals, issues, events, topics, and their attributes" (Liu, 2012, p. 7).

Automatic sentiment analysis is an area in continuous development. It first started with the identification of subjectivity (Wiebe, 2000) and, after that, polarity identification and measurement of strength have become the center of new developments (Turney, 2002). The objectives of sentiment analysis are evolving as well, as different types of information are used. For instance, initially, entity- and aspect-based information was used (Hu and Liu, 2004) but, later, new types of information, such as discourse structure information, have been used (Polanyi and Zaenen, 2006).[1]

This study is the first work that examines lexical and discourse structure information for sentiment analysis of Basque. The main aim is to evaluate which discourse structures can help in polarity detection following a lexicon-based approach. Our hypothesis is that some discourse structures are more related to opinions than others and we want to identify and study how they can help in a sentiment analysis task.

The paper is organized as follows: Section 2 discusses related works. Section 3 explains the methodology of the study and Section 4 presents the results and error analysis. Finally, conclusions and future work are given in Section 5.

2 Related Work

Various studies from different theoretical approaches analyze the influence of nuclearity and some rhetorical relations in sentiment analysis tasks. For example, Zhou et al. (2011) use discursive in-

---

[1] See a detailed review of sentiment analysis in Taboada (2016).

Proceedings of the 6th Workshop Recent Advances in RST and Related Formalisms, pages 39–47,
Santiago de Compostela, Spain, September 4 2017. ©2017 Association for Computational Linguistics

formation in Chinese to eliminate noise at the intra-sentence level, improving not only polarity classification but also the labeling of rhetorical relations at sentence level.

Wu and Qiu (2012) analyze sentiment analysis based on Rhetorical Structure Theory (RST) (Mann and Thompson, 1988) in Chinese texts. They split texts in segments and, then, they train weights taking into account relations and nuclearity, showing that CONTRAST, CAUSE, CONDITION and GENERALIZATION have a more important role in this task than other discourse relations. Bhatia et al. (2015) use a simpler classification of relations into CONTRAST or NON-CONTRAST, and they show that the distinction improves the results of bag-of-words classifiers using Rhetorical Recursive Neural Networks.

Chardon et al. (2013) rate documents using three approaches: i) bag-of-words, ii) partial discourse information and iii) full discourse information. The discursive approach gives the best result in the framework of Segmented Discursive Representation Theory (SDRT).

Trnavac et al. (2016) propose that a few rhetorical relations have a significant effect on polarity: CONCESSION, CONTRAST, EVALUATION and RESULT. They also conclude that nuclei tend to contain more evaluative words than satellites.

Alkorta et al. (2015) analyze which features perform better in order to detect the polarity of texts using machine learning techniques on Basque texts. Their results show that discourse structure is needed to improve results along with other types of features. They use a dictionary created by automatic means with an unsupervised method (Vicente et al., 2017). The dictionary values of their work are binary (-1 for negative polarity and $+1$ for a positive one).

In this work, we analyze which coherence relations could help to improve lexicon-based sentiment analysis, so that we can assign different weights to discourse structures following Bhatia et al. (2015) when calculating sentiment analysis for a whole text. For this task, we use the RST framework.

The main contributions of this work are: i) A fine-grained dictionary, manually created for Basque with 5 different negative values and 5 different positive ones, ranging from -5 to $+5$. ii) A study of how discourse structure interacts with this polarity lexicon.

3　Methodology

The subsections below detail the main steps followed in the present study.

3.1　Extraction of discourse structures

In the first phase, different discourse structures were compared. They will be used to determine which ones can be helpful in sentiment analysis. To extract as many discourse structures as possible, we use the corpus described in Alkorta et al. (2016), annotated for discourse relations according to RST.

The corpus contains 29 book reviews. Regarding polarity, it is a balanced corpus, with 14 positive reviews and 15 negative ones. The majority of reviews were collected from a website specialized in Basque literary reviews (Kritiken Hemeroteka).[2]

The following subcorpora were created, following some discourse constraints:

— Full text, containing all the RS-tree of the text.

— Texts extracted from central units (CU)[3] of the text.

— Text spans extracted from the CU of the text and from the central subconstituent (CS)[4] of some rhetorical relations (see Table 1).

Relation	CS	Relation	CS
ELABORATION	34	CONCESSION	2
EVALUATION	32	RESTATEMENT	2
PREPARATION	32	SUMMARY	2
BACKGROUND	13	ANTITHESIS	1
CIRCUMSTANCE	8	PURPOSE	1
INTERPRETATION	6	MOTIVATION	1
CAUSE	4	JUSTIFY	1

Table 1: Number of central subconstituents (CS) in the corpus per relation type linked to the CU.

We extracted 139 instances of rhetorical relations from our corpus. For some relations, such as ELABORATION and PREPARATION (66 of 139), we do

---

[2] http://kritikak.armiarma.eus/.

[3] Central units are defined as the most important EDU (Elementary Discourse Unit), and it is the main nucleus when tree structure is constructed (Iruskieta, 2014).

[4] Central subconstituents are "the most important unit of the modifier span that is the most important unit of the satellite span" (Iruskieta et al., 2015, p. 5).

not expect them to contain important polarity information, because these relations only add extra information to the central unit. In fact, Mann and Thompson (1988, p. 273) mention that in the case of ELABORATION "R(eader) recognized the situation presented in S(atellite) as providing additional detail for N(uclei). R(eader) identifies the element of subject matter for which detail is provided". Similarly, in PREPARATION "R(eader) is more ready, interested or oriented for reading N(uclei)". We did not take into account relations with low frequency (a single instance), such as MOTIVATION, JUSTIFICATION, ANTITHESIS and PURPOSE. Consequently, we will work with a subcorpus containing 69 relations, where almost half of them are central subconstituents of EVALUATION.[5]

3.2 Polarity extraction and evaluation

Polarity was extracted from all the discourse structures using a dictionary (v1.0) of words annotated with their semantic orientation: polarity (positive or negative) and strength (from 1 to 5). To do so, the Spanish SO-CAL dictionary (Taboada et al., 2011) was translated using the Elhuyar (Zerbitzuak, 2013) and Zehazki (Sarasola, 2005) bilingual Spanish-Basque dictionaries. Our dictionary contains information about grammatical categories: nouns, adjectives, verbs and adverbs.

Dictionary	Words	SO(-)	SO(+)
Nouns	2,882	1,635	1,247
Adjectives	3,162	1,733	1,429
Adverbs	652	225	427
Verbs	1,657	1,006	651
Total	**8,353**	**4,599**	**3,754**

Table 2: Characteristics of the Basque dictionary.

As Table (2) shows, the dictionary contains a total of 8,353 words. The majority of words are nouns

[5] All the reviews of the corpus were coded, assigning the domain LIB (for literature review) and a number, and each discourse structure extracted from them was also coded: CU stands for text that only contains the central unit of the text, CAUS for texts that contain CAUSE relation, INT for INTERPRETATION, ELAB for ELABORATION, CIR for CIRCUMSTANCE, BACK for BACKGROUND and finally, EVA for EVALUATION. In addition, if the same relation appears more than once in each text, we added letters (e.g., a, b, c) to each relation, to indicate their order of appearance.

and adjectives. In terms of polarity, there are more negative words (almost one thousand more).

We created a polarity tagger, based on this dictionary. The polarity tagger used the output of Eustagger (Aduriz et al., 2003), which is a robust and wide-coverage morphological analyzer and a Part-of-Speech tagger (POS) for Basque, to enrich the text with a POS analysis information and to assign polarity to every lemma of the dictionary that matches with the lemma and category of the text. With the aim of comparing the results of the system, a linguist annotated the polarity (positive, negative or neutral) of all the discourse structures described in Section (3.1).

Figure 1 shows a portion of the RST tree of one text (LIB28).[6] After the full RST analysis was performed for each text, we extracted the following discourse structures: i) the text of the central unit (EDU_2), as shown in Example (1), and ii) the central subconstituent of the EVALUATION ($EDU_{21,22,23,25}$), in Example (2).

(1) XIX. mendean Gasteiz inguruak izutu$_{(-3)}$ zituen Juan Diaz de Garaio Sacamantecas pertsonaia hartu$_{(+2)}$ du Aitor Aranak (Legazpi, 1963) bere azken eleberrian$_{(+2)}$. (LIB28_CU)
English: Aitor Arana (Legazpi, 1963) has taken$_{(+2)}$ in his last novel$_{(+2)}$ the character Juan Diaz Garaio Sacamantecas who scared$_{(-3)}$ the surroundings of Gasteiz in the 19th century.

(2) Hala ere, nahiko$_{(+2)}$ planoa da nobela$_{(+2)}$, erritmoa falta$_{(-1)}$ zaio eta bortxaketen kontaketak aspergarriak$_{(-3)}$ ere bihurtzen$_{(-2)}$ dira, Bestalde, alabaren ikuspuntua$_{(+2)}$ ez da batere argi geratzen$_{(-2)}$, (...). (LIB28_EVA)
English: However, the novel$_{(+2)}$ is fairly$_{(+2)}$ flat, it lacks$_{(-1)}$ rhythm, and the stories of rapes also become$_{(-2)}$ boring$_{(-3)}$. On the other hand, the point of view$_{(+2)}$ of the daughter is not clear$_{(-2)}$ (...)

The classifier then assigns polarity to each word in the dictionary, as shown in Table 3 and in examples (1) and (2). The table shows that the semantic

[6] Size constraints prevent us from showing the entire tree.

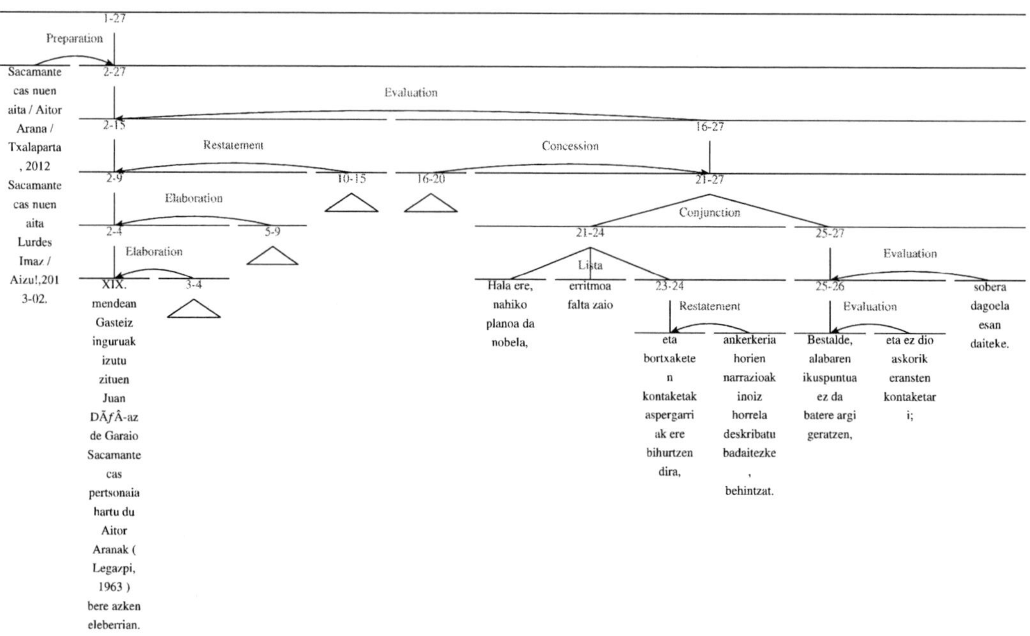

Figure 1: Central unit and the central subconstituent of EVALUATION in text LIB28

orientation of the central unit (LIB28_cu) is positive, while the semantic orientation of the central subconstituent (LIB28_EVA) is negative.

Ex.	CS ID	Classifier	SO	Manual
1	LIB28_cu	$-3+2+2$	$+1$	Neutral
2	LIB28_EVA	$+2+2-1-3-2$	-2	Negative

Table 3: Semantic orientation of LIB28_cu and LIB28_EVA: results of the classifier and of the manual annotation.

3.3 Normalization of semantic orientation results

We normalized the results obtained with the classifier to compare the different discourse structures, as in the following examples:

(3) Gure izaeraz$_{(+3)}$ hausnartzeko$_{(+1)}$ manual gisa eta, etxetik ibiltzeko$_{(+2)}$ dosi psikoanalitiko ttipi$_{(-1)}$ moduan$_{(+1)}$ hautematen$_{(+4)}$ dut nik. (LIB26_INT)
English: I consider$_{(+4)}$ it is like a manual with a small$_{(-1)}$ dose of psychoanalysis, a domestic$_{(+2)}$ consideration$_{(+1)}$ to reflect about$_{(+1)}$ our being$_{(+3)}$.

(4) Nolanahi$_{(-2)}$ den dela, saihestezina da gatazka$_{(-4)}$. (LIB13_CIR)
English: In any case$_{(-2)}$, the conflict$_{(-4)}$ is inevitable.

The results obtained by the classifier are $+112$ (LIB10),[7] $+10$ (LIB26_INT) and -6 (LIB23_CIR), as shown in Table 4. To compare those results among them, we normalized the frequencies dividing these results by the number of the words in each discourse structure. We show the normalized frequencies in Table 4.

Ex.	CS ID	SO	Words	NV
3	LIB10	$+112$	418	$+0.27$
	LIB26_INT	$+10$	17	$+0.59$
4	LIB13_CIR	-6	8	-0.75

Table 4: Examples of semantic orientation results after normalization (NV = Normalized Value).

Table 4 shows how normalization helps to better adjust the weight of the automatically assigned polarities. As a matter of fact, the values are adjusted

[7] Remember that this notation, LIB10, represents the entire text.

to a smaller range and, therefore, they are more easily comparable.

4 Results and error analysis

The results show that using a simple classifier with a manually built dictionary, along with different rhetorical structures, helps to identify the strength of such structures. For example, the result obtained in the central subconstituent of EVALUATION is strong.

(5) Guztiz$_{(+3)}$ gomendagarria$_{(+3)}$.
(LIB26_EVA)
English: Highly$_{(+3)}$ recommended$_{(+3)}$.

(6) Liburu$_{(+5)}$ sano gomendagarria$_{(+3)}$ da,
(LIB23d_EVA)
English: It's a very recommendable$_{(+3)}$ book$_{(+5)}$,

In Examples (5) and (6) the strength is higher than 1: +2 (+6 / 3 = 2) and +1.6 (+8 / 5 = +1.6), respectively, while the strength in other relations is lower.

(7) Izugarri$_{(+5)}$ gustura irakurri dut Bertol Arrietaren Alter ero narrazio bilduma. (LIB26_CAUS)
English: I have read very$_{(+5)}$ comfortable the Alter ero narration collection of Bertol Arrieta.

(8) Udako giro$_{(-2)}$ sapa horretan gertatzen diren kontakizun xumeak$_{(+3)}$ ekarriko dizkigu idazleak. (LIB15_CIR)
English: The writer will bring us the common$_{(+3)}$ stories that happen in that sticky atmosphere$_{(-2)}$ of summer.

The strength of CAUSE shows in Example (7) a value lower than 1 (+5 / 11 = +0.45). In Example (8) the central subconstituent of INTERPRETATION shows a value lower that 1 with a value of +0.08 (+1 / 12 = +0.08) and lower value than in Example (7).

We have analyzed the discourse structure with the aim of determining the strongest discourse structures of our corpus and therefore the structures that contribute most to improving sentiment labeling.

Most of the values are between −1 and +1, but in 11.59% of the relations (8 of 69 relations), the values are higher than one (see Table 5).

RR	Total	Total (<1)	%
EVALUATION	32	6	18.75
INTERPRETATION	6	1	16.67
BACKGROUND	13	1	7.69
Others	18	0	0.00
Total	69	8	11.59

Table 5: Polarity strength ($< +1$ and > -1) of central subconstituents.

The most frequent and strongest value is obtained in EVALUATION (18.75%, 6 of 32). After that, the second strongest relation is INTERPRETATION with 16.67% (1 of 6). And, finally, BACKGROUND is once above one (7.69%, 1 of 13).

As examples (9, 10, 11, 12, 13) show, these relations have similar characteristics: short central subconstituents with many and strong evaluative words.

(9) berriz, zuzenean$_{(+3)}$ egin$_{(+2)}$ dut. (LIB14a_EVA)
English: whereas, I have done$_{(+2)}$ it directly$_{(+3)}$.

(10) Abentura$_{(+2)}$ liburu$_{(+5)}$ ederra$_{(+3)}$ iruditu$_{(+1)}$ zait, eta erremate paregabea$_{(+4)}$ trilogiarentzat. (LIB14b_EVA)
English: It seemed$_{(+2)}$ to me a beautiful$_{(+3)}$ adventure$_{(+2)}$ book$_{(+5)}$, and extraordinary$_{(+4)}$ finish for the trilogy.

(11) izenburua zuzen$_{(+3)}$ jarrita$_{(+1)}$, (LIB29a_EVA)
English: the title set$_{(+1)}$ correctly$_{(+3)}$,

(12) Intrigazko$_{(+2)}$ argumentua garatu$_{(+1)}$ nahi$_{(+3)}$ da. (LIB01b_EVA)
English: You want$_{(+3)}$ to develop$_{(+1)}$ an argument of intrigue$_{(+2)}$.

(13) Folklorean ikusi$_{(+4)}$ nahi$_{(+3)}$ ditu idazleak komunitate$_{(+1)}$ baten bizi$_{(+2)}$ nahi$_{(+3)}$ eta indarra$_{(+3)}$. (LIB35_INT)
English: The author wants$_{(+3)}$ to see$_{(+4)}$ in the folklore the strength$_{(+3)}$ and the desire$_{(+3)}$ to live$_{(+2)}$ of one community$_{(+1)}$.

Consequently, their value is higher than one, as shown in Table (6).

Ex.	CS ID	NV
9	LIB14a_EVA	1
10	LIB14b_EVA	1.36
11	LIB29a_EVA	1
12	LIB01b_EVA	1
13	LIB35_INT	1.33

Table 6: Central subconstituents and their value ($<$ +1).

In contrast, we did not see any case of other central subconstituents with a value higher than one. If we compare partial discourse structures with the results obtained with all words of a text, the strength is lower in all cases. This is because polarity words do not have the same frequency in other rhetorical relations and, as a consequence, the concentration of words with semantic orientation is smaller. The highest value across the texts is $+0.50$ (LIB35), and the lowest value is -0.1 (LIB28).

These results suggest that opinions and, consequently, words with semantic orientation, are mainly found in the central subconstituent of EVALUATION, INTERPRETATION and BACKGROUND.

Apart from helping to identify the strongest central subconstituents, we have observed that the dictionary together with some central subconstituents can help in sentiment analysis. In fact, assigning a weight to some CSs could help to improve sentiment analysis results, as in text LIB34.

(14) ”Behi eroak$_{(-3)}$” bilduman, ordea, egileak aurrekoan izan zituen arazoak$_{(-1)}$ konpondu$_{(+3)}$ ditu. Zoritxarrez$_{(-4)}$ bilduma honek batzuetan xelebrekeria$_{(-1)}$ merketik$_{(+3)}$ badu nahiko$_{(-2)}$. (LIB34b_EVA)
English: However, in ”Behi eroak$_{(-3)}$” collection, the author has solved$_{(+3)}$ the problems$_{(-1)}$ that he had before. Unfortunately$_{(-4)}$, this collection has enough$_{(-2)}$ cheap$_{(+3)}$ eccentricity$_{(-1)}$.

The human annotator marked LIB34 as a negative review and the system assigns a value of $+0.15$ for the entire text, but a negative value of -0.2 ($-5/25=-0.2$) for LIB34b_EVA, Example (14). If the proper weight was assigned to this CS (LIB34b_EVA), the semantic positive orientation of the entire text (LIB34) would be corrected and tagged as negative.

We analyzed the previous finding in all the CSs of EVALUATION, but taking the results of the human annotator, instead of the classifier. In total, in 29 texts, there are 32 CSs of EVALUATION and in 24 of them, the human annotation of polarity of CSs and texts agree. So, the agreement happens in 75% of CSs and 86.20% of texts (25 texts).

Even though most of the times there is agreement between the annotated polarity of CSs and texts, this does not happen in all cases. For example, in other cases, the same text has one positive central subconstituent and another negative central subconstituent of EVALUATION. These cases are 12.50% of central subconstituents and 6.89% of texts (LIB03ab and LIB12ab).

Finally, there are two cases in which the polarity of the central subconstituent of EVALUATION and the polarity of all text are the opposite (LIB02ab and LIB19ab).

(15) eta apustu ausarta$_{(+3)}$ egin$_{(+2)}$ du bertan. (LIB19a_EVA)
English: and has made$_{(+2)}$ a strong$_{(+3)}$ bet there.

(16) Batetik, idazleak goi-literaturaren jokalekua hautatu duelako —liburuaren$_{(+5)}$ erlazio estratestualak eta baliatutako$_{(+1)}$ errekurtso andana$_{(-1)}$ lekuko—. Bestetik, borgestarretik asko duen jokoa$_{(-4)}$ delako liburuan$_{(+5)}$ dagoena. (LIB19b_EVA)
English: On the one hand, because the writer has chosen a scene from high literature —extratextual relations and a lot$_{(-1)}$ of resources used$_{(+1)}$ in the book$_{(+5)}$ as proof—. On the other hand, because there is a game$_{(-4)}$ that has a lot of Borges in the book$_{(+5)}$.

In this case, the text LIB19 is negative, whereas examples (15) and (16) are positive. We observe that the change of polarity happens in the EVALUATION situated inside an ELABORATION coherence relation.

(17) Baina, horiek horrela izanik ere, emaitza$_{(+1)}$ zalantzagarria$_{(-1)}$ da. Izan ere, liter-

aturan, baliabide$_{(+2)}$ orok medio izan behar$_{(-1)}$ du, eta irakurleak ikusi$_{(+4)}$ behar$_{(-1)}$ du errekurtsoak literaturaren mesedetan$_{(+3)}$ daudela "baita metaliteraturaz ari$_{(+2)}$ garenean ere". Hemen, ordea, medioak emaitza$_{(+1)}$ estaltzen$_{(-2)}$ du maiz$_{(+1)}$: literaturaren mekanismoekin egindako$_{(+2)}$ jokoek$_{(-4)}$ ipuinetan$_{(+2)}$ dauden istorioak$_{(-1)}$ indartu$_{(+1)}$ beharrean$_{(-1)}$, higatu$_{(-2)}$ egiten$_{(+2)}$ dituzte. Aldamioa oso$_{(+1)}$ nabarmena$_{(+4)}$ da, idazle askok beretzat nahi$_{(+3)}$ lukeen ahalmenez$_{(+2)}$ jasoa$_{(+2)}$. Haatik, hartatik sortzen$_{(+2)}$ den literatura ez da hain ikusgarria$_{(+4)}$. (LIB19_ELAB)

English: But, they being so, the result$_{(+1)}$ is doubtful$_{(-1)}$. In fact, in the literature, all resources$_{(+2)}$ need$_{(-1)}$ to be the medium, and the reader needs$_{(-1)}$ to see$_{(+4)}$ that resources are in favor$_{(+3)}$ of literary, "also when we are talking$_{(+2)}$ about metaliterature." But here, the medium hides$_{(-2)}$ the result$_{(+1)}$ in many times$_{(+1)}$: games$_{(-4)}$ made$_{(+2)}$ by literary devices wear away$_{(+2)(-2)}$ the tales$_{(-1)}$ of the stories$_{(+2)}$ instead$_{(-1)}$ of strengthening$_{(+1)}$ them. The scaffolding is very$_{(+1)}$ evident$_{(+4)}$, built$_{(+2)}$ with capacity$_{(+2)}$ as many writers would like$_{(+3)}$. However, the literature created$_{(+2)}$ is not very impressive$_{(+4)}$.

In Example (17), there are some discourse markers (*but, however*) and words (*doubtful, wear away, not very impressive*) that suggest a change of polarity that affects all text. Consequently, this example shows that, apart from central constituents of EVALUATION, a deeper analysis of nuclearity assigning different weighs could be necessary in order to improve sentiment analysis.

4.1 Error analysis

In this section, we will analyze the errors that can affect accurate detection of sentiment analysis, and specially the ones that were relevant in this study: *i*) errors in negative reviews, and *ii*) errors related to syntax.

4.1.1 Errors in negative reviews

Brooke et al. (2009) mention that lexicon-based sentiment classifiers show a positive bias because humans tend to use positive language (see also Taboada et al. (2017)). We also found this problem by examining the results of the classifier.

As Table (2) shows, the majority of the words in the dictionary are negative. Therefore, it is expected that we will detect more negative words in the texts. However, the results of the classifier with our dictionary show a tendency to classify texts as positive in different discourse structures of the texts.

For example, this tendency is observed in results of the CS of EVALUATION[8] (see Table 7).

CS of EVALUATION	Total	Guess	%
Positive	20	19	95.00
Negative	11	4	36.36
Neutral	1	0	0.00
Total	32	23	71.88

Table 7: Positive polarity tendency in central sub-constituents of EVALUATION.

Table 7 demonstrates that the classifier tends to consider as positive the majority of central subconstituents of this rhetorical relation. In fact, 26 of 32 central subconstituents have been classified as positive. Consequently, the correct guess rate in CSs is higher in positive (95%) versus negative (36.36%).

A tendency to positive semantic orientation is higher if we analyze the results of all texts instead of just central subconstituents of EVALUATION as shown in Table 8.

Texts	Total	Guess	%
Positive	14	14	100
Negative	15	1	6.67
Total	29	15	51.72

Table 8: Positive polarity tendency in texts of the corpus.

As a consequence of this positive bias, our classifier guesses easily the texts with positive polarity and the correct guess rate is 100%. In contrast, the rate is very low in negative texts, as a matter of fact, there is only one right guess in text LIB28 (-0.1) and consequently, the correct guess rate is 6.67%.

---

[8]We have analyzed this relation and not others because it accounts for almost half of all the studied rhetorical relations.

However, if we compare the results of central sub-constituents and texts, we can observe another tendency. The rate of correct assignments in positive texts is higher (95% vs. 100%) on the full texts (long text), while for negatives it is higher (36.36% vs. 6.67%) in central subconstituents (short text). This suggests that the tendency to positive semantic orientation is stronger using our dictionary as a bag-of-words approach as the text is longer.

In summary, the dictionary classifier shows the same problem already described in previous research, as there is a strong tendency towards positive semantic orientation, which increases as the text is longer.

4.1.2   Errors related to syntax

As we mentioned in Section 4.1.1, there is a tendency towards positive polarity caused by the use of positive language and, for that reason, the correct guess rate is lower in negative texts. However, it is not the only reason, and information at the syntactic level also affects the results. As an example, we will discuss one particular problem, negation. Due to negation, the polarity of a sentence is changed and it is necessary to take this characteristic into account in sentiment analysis.

> (18)   (...)   narrazioak ere <u>ez</u> du arretarik bereganatzen$_{(+4)}$ (...) (LIB18_EVA).
> English: (...) the narration also does <u>not</u> get attention$_{(+4)}$ (...)

In Example (18), the semantic orientation of the sentence would be negative but our classifier regards it as positive. The classifier has detected *bereganatu* 'to get hold of' as a positive word ($+4/7=+0.57$). But, in this case, a correct analysis should assign it a negative value.

In a first study of our subcorpus of CSs of different rhetorical relations, we estimate that this affects to 11.43% of the constituents, since 8 of 70 CSs have some type of negation.

5   Conclusions and future work

This study has analyzed whether combining a semantic oriented dictionary with some discourse structure constraints is helpful in sentiment analysis of Basque.

The results show that i) the central subconstituents (CS) of EVALUATION, INTERPRETATION and BACKGROUND are the units with the strongest semantic orientation, and ii) the CSs of EVALUATION could help in improving semantic orientation of the texts, given that the results of the human annotation of polarity of CSs and the full text text agree in 75% of the cases.

On the other hand, error analysis has shown that there are some aspects that should be addressed: i) a tendency to positive semantic orientation, and ii) sentence and more discourse level constraints are needed.

In the near future, we plan to pursue the following aspects:

i) Do reviews have a specific discourse structure? We hypothesize that reviews have a specific structure and, consequently, the same discourse relations will be repeated with high frequency, and they will appear in the same place.

ii) How we can weigh properly the central subconstituents of EVALUATION and INTERPRETATION, and neutralize the positive tendency, to improve the results for negative reviews?

iii) Are other CSs not linked to the CU important for sentiment analysis?

Acknowledgments

We thank Arantxa Otegi for assistance with the lexicon-based polarity tagger. Jon Alkorta's work is funded by a PhD grant (PRE_2016_2_0153) from the Basque Government and Mikel Iruskieta's work is funded by the TUNER project (TIN2015-65308-C5-1-R) funded by the Spanish *Ministerio de Economia, Comercio y Competitividad*.

References

[Aduriz et al.2003] Itziar Aduriz, Izaskun Aldezabal, Inaki Alegria, J Arriola, Arantza Dıaz de Ilarraza, Nerea Ezeiza, and Koldo Gojenola. 2003. Finite state applications for basque. In *EACL2003 Workshop on Finite-State Methods in Natural Language Processing*, pages 3–11.

[Alkorta et al.2015] Jon Alkorta, Koldo Gojenola, Mikel Iruskieta, and Alicia Prez. 2015. Using relational discourse structure information in basque sentiment analysis. In *SEPLN 5th Workshop RST and Discourse Studies. ISBN: 978-84-608-1989-9. https://gplsi.dlsi.ua.es/sepln15/en/node/63.*

[Alkorta et al.2016] Jon Alkorta, Koldo Gojenola, and MIkel Iruskieta. 2016. Creating and evaluating a polarity - balanced corpus for basque sentiment analysis. In *IWoDA16 Fourth International Workshop on Discourse Analysis. Santiago de Compostela , September 29 th - 30 th . Extended Abstracts. ISBN: 978 - 84 - 608 - 9305 - 9.*

[Bhatia et al.2015] Parminder Bhatia, Yangfeng Ji, and Jacob Eisenstein. 2015. Better document-level sentiment analysis from rst discourse parsing. *arXiv preprint arXiv:1509.01599.*

[Brooke et al.2009] Julian Brooke, Milan Tofiloski, and Maite Taboada. 2009. Cross-linguistic sentiment analysis: From english to spanish. In *RANLP*, pages 50–54.

[Chardon et al.2013] Baptiste Chardon, Farah Benamara, Yannick Mathieu, Vladimir Popescu, and Nicholas Asher. 2013. Measuring the effect of discourse structure on sentiment analysis. In *International Conference on Intelligent Text Processing and Computational Linguistics*, pages 25–37. Springer.

[Hu and Liu2004] Minqing Hu and Bing Liu. 2004. Mining and summarizing customer reviews. In *Proceedings of the tenth ACM SIGKDD international conference on Knowledge discovery and data mining*, pages 168–177. ACM.

[Iruskieta et al.2015] Mikel Iruskieta, Iria Da Cunha, and Maite Taboada. 2015. A qualitative comparison method for rhetorical structures: identifying different discourse structures in multilingual corpora. *Language resources and evaluation*, 49(2):263–309.

[Iruskieta2014] Mikel Iruskieta. 2014. Pragmatikako erlaziozko diskurtso-egitura: deskribapena eta bere ebaluazioa hizkuntzalaritza komputazionalean (a description of pragmatics rhetorical structure and its evaluation in computational linguistic). *Doktore-tesia. EHU, informatika Fakultatea.*

[Liu2012] Bing Liu. 2012. Sentiment analysis and opinion mining. *Synthesis lectures on human language technologies*, 5(1):1–167.

[Mann and Thompson1988] William C Mann and Sandra A Thompson. 1988. Rhetorical structure theory: Toward a functional theory of text organization. *Text-Interdisciplinary Journal for the Study of Discourse*, 8(3):243–281.

[Polanyi and Zaenen2006] Livia Polanyi and Annie Zaenen. 2006. Contextual valence shifters. In *Computing attitude and affect in text: Theory and applications*, pages 1–10. Springer.

[Sarasola2005] Ibon Sarasola. 2005. *Zehazki: gaztelania-euskara hiztegia.* Alberdania.

[Taboada et al.2011] Maite Taboada, Julian Brooke, Milan Tofiloski, Kimberly Voll, and Manfred Stede. 2011. Lexicon-based methods for sentiment analysis. *Computational linguistics*, 37(2):267–307.

[Taboada et al.2017] Maite Taboada, Radoslava Trnavac, and Cliff Goddard. 2017. On being negative. *Corpus Pragmatics*, 1(1):57–76.

[Taboada2016] Maite Taboada. 2016. Sentiment analysis: an overview from linguistics. *Annual Review of Linguistics*, 2:325–347.

[Trnavac et al.2016] Radoslava Trnavac, Debopam Das, and Maite Taboada. 2016. Discourse relations and evaluation. *Corpora*, 11(2):169–190.

[Turney2002] Peter D Turney. 2002. Thumbs up or thumbs down?: semantic orientation applied to unsupervised classification of reviews. In *Proceedings of the 40th annual meeting on association for computational linguistics*, pages 417–424. Association for Computational Linguistics.

[Vicente et al.2017] Inaki San Vicente, Rodrigo Agerri, and German Rigau. 2017. Q-wordnet ppv: Simple, robust and (almost) unsupervised generation of polarity lexicons for multiple languages. *arXiv preprint arXiv:1702.01711.*

[Wiebe2000] Janyce Wiebe. 2000. Learning subjective adjectives from corpora. In *AAAI/IAAI*, pages 735–740.

[Wu and Qiu2012] Fei Wang1 Yunfang Wu and Likun Qiu. 2012. Exploiting discourse relations for sentiment analysis. In *24th International Conference on Computational Linguistics*, page 1311.

[Zerbitzuak2013] Elhuyar Hizkuntza Zerbitzuak. 2013. Elhuyar hiztegia: euskara-gaztelania, castellano-vasco. usurbil: Elhuyar.

[Zhou et al.2011] Lanjun Zhou, Binyang Li, Wei Gao, Zhongyu Wei, and Kam-Fai Wong. 2011. Unsupervised discovery of discourse relations for eliminating intra-sentence polarity ambiguities. In *Proceedings of the Conference on Empirical Methods in Natural Language Processing*, pages 162–171. Association for Computational Linguistics.

Framework for the Analysis of Simplified Texts
Taking Discourse into Account: the Basque Causal Relations as Case Study

Itziar Gonzalez-Dios and **Arantza Diaz de Ilarraza** and **Mikel Iruskieta**
itziar.gonzalezd@ehu.eus; a.diazdeilarraza@ehu.eus, mikel.iruskieta@ehu.eus
University of the Basque Country (UPV/EHU)
IXA Group for NLP
Manuel Lardizabal pasealekua 1. 20018 Donostia, Gipuzkoa

Abstract

Text simplification is crucial for some readers
to understand the content of a text. Analyzing
simplified texts can help to understand the mechanism hidden in the process of simplification. In
this paper we present a research framework to
analyze the impact of simplification operations on
discourse. To that end, we used the Corpus of the
Simplified Basque texts (CBST) and we studied
the strategies followed in the simplification of
causal relations and their effects at discourse
level. From this analysis of the sample we derive
that discourse has not been always taken into
account which may lead to a lack of coherence
in the simplified text.

1   Introduction and Related Work

Text Simplification is a research line that has been
important in the educational community (Simensen,
1987; Young, 1999; Crossley et al., 2007) but it is also
becoming important in the Natural Language Processing (NLP) community. Therefore, multidisciplinary
researchers are working on different ways to make text
simplification by automatic or semi-automatic means.
This task is known as Automatic or Automated Text
Simplification (ATS) and its development has been
deeply explained in the literature ((Saggion, 2017)).

In this work, we want to describe a framework to
analyze simplified texts taking discourse structure
following the Rhetorical Structure Theory (RST)[1]
(Mann and Thompson, 1988) into account and answer
the following research questions:

— How can we describe the impact of simplification
operations in discourse?

— How do simplification operations affect the
rhetorical structures of the original texts?

This type of studies need annotated corpora which are
expensive, but at the same time, necessary. We can find
in the literature corpora available for English (Petersen
and Ostendorf, 2007; Xu et al., 2015; Pellow and
Eskenazi, 2014), Danish (Klerke and Søgaard, 2012),
German (Klaper et al., 2013), Brazilian Portuguese
(Caseli et al., 2009), Spanish (Bott and Saggion,
2011), Italian (Brunato et al., 2015) and Basque
(Gonzalez-Dios, 2016). In the case of the last three
corpora, simplification operations have been annotated
and general annotation schemes derived.   Besides,
from the simplification perspective, Gonzalez-Dios
et al. (2016) analyzed in the Basque corpus whether
conditional, concessive, purpose, temporal and relative
clauses[2] have been simplified or not, and if so, which
were the macro-operations that had been performed.

From the discourse perspective, Crossley et al. (2007)
analyzed the cohesion of 105 texts taken from seven
texts-books aiming beginners of English as a second
language with Coh-metrix (Graesser et al., 2004). They
focused on the following seven sets: i) causal cohesion,
ii) connectives and logical operators, iii) coreference
measures, iv) density of major parts of speech measures,
v) polysemy and hypernymy measures, vi) syntactic
complexity, and vii) word information and frequency
measures. They found out among others that original

---

[1]RST is an approach to describe text coherence by means of
coherence relations or rhetorical relations and has been applied to
many NLP tasks.

[2]These clauses are the most five predictive features for the
readability assessment system for Basque (Gonzalez-Dios et al.,
2014) at the syntactic level.

Proceedings of the 6th Workshop Recent Advances in RST and Related Formalisms, pages 48–57,
Santiago de Compostela, Spain, September 4 2017. ©2017 Association for Computational Linguistics

Original	Structural	Intuitive
Beraz, hegoaren formak, nahiz eta hegan egitearen lehen arrazoia ez izan, garrantzi handia du, inguruan duen airearen jarioan asko eragiten duelako.	*Beraz, hegoaren formak garrantzi handia du* [;] *izan ere, hegoaren formak inguruan duen airearen jarioan asko eragiten du* [.] *Hegoaren forma, ordea, ez da hegan egitearen lehen arrazoia.*	*Beraz, hegoaren formak, nahiz eta hegan egitearen lehen arrazoia ez izan, garrantzi handia du* [;] *izan ere, inguruan duen airearen jarioan asko eragiten du.*
So, the form of the wings, though it is not the main motive of the flying, is very important, because it affects a lot the surrounding air flow.	So, the form of the wings is very important; indeed, the form of the wings affects a lot the surrounding air flow. The form of the wings is not, however, the main motive of the flying.'	So, the form of the wings, though it is not the main motive of the flying, is very important; indeed, it affects a lot the surrounding air flow.

Table 1: The original sentence Bernoulli_80 and its two simplified versions

texts had a higher ratio of causal verbs to causal particles. Therefore, original texts exhibited less causal relations. In the analysis of intuitively simplified texts, Crossley et al. (2012) found out that advanced level texts exhibited less causal cohesion than beginning level texts.

To our knowledge, there is no joint framework to analyze simplified texts taking simplification operations and discourse into account. That is why the aim of this paper is to propose a framework to measure how simplification operations affect relational discourse structure. In this study, we focus on forms used to express causality because reducing causal discourse relations is crucial for people with language disorders. For example, Kong et al. (2017) stated that the coherence of speakers with aphasia tended to miss essential information content. This can be measured because aphasia speakers reduce some RST relations, such as ELABORATION and causal relations in their speech.

This paper is structured as follows: in Section 2 we present the resources needed to perform the analysis; in Section 3, we describe the framework for the analysis; in Section 4, we present the results of the quantitative analysis on the causal relations and in Section 5, we conclude and outline the future work.

2 Resources

In order to perform this study, we have used the Corpus of Basque Simplified Text (CBST). This corpus is a collection of texts divided in 227 sentences of the science popularisation domain. Each original sentence in the corpus has a structurally simplified and an intuitively simplified sentence. In this corpus, the operations

performed in order to simplify the sentences have been annotated following an annotation scheme[3] composed by the following eight macro-operations: i) delete, ii) merge, iii) split, iv) transformation, v) insert, vi) reordering, vii) no operation and $viii$) other. These macro-operations involve many operations (Gonzalez-Dios, 2016). In Table 1 we show the original sentence identified as *Bernoulli_80* and its two simplified versions.

To create the cause subcorpus, we extracted semi-automatically the causal clauses as done by Gonzalez-Dios et al. (2016) and then, following the proposal of Iruskieta et al. (2016), we extracted the sentences containing causal discourse markers and causal lexical signals. The main figures of this sample are presented in Table 2.

	Original	Structural	Intuitive
Sentences	69	90	97
Words	1441	1482	1399

Table 2: Sentence and word number in our sample

The number of causal structures found in the original sentences of the CBST is shown according to their type in Table 3: i) syntactically marked causal signals (syntactic), ii) causal signals made explicit by discourse markers (DMs), iii) causal relations signaled with

---

[3] Note that annotation results may yield subjective idiosyncrasies, due to fact that the corpus is annotated only with one annotator. In our opinion this fact is not a problem for the aim of this paper, because our objective is to explore a methodology to measure a joint analysis between simplification and relational discourse structure. As far as we know, no agreement measures have been given in the annotation process of simplified corpora.

nouns and verbs (Lexical).

Type	Simp.	RST	Joint
Syntactic	17	3	3
DMs	16	3	3
Lexical	32	3	3

Table 3: Number of analyzed causal structures

The additional resources used in this analysis are 1) a study of the frequencies and positions of the adverbial clauses (Gonzalez-Dios et al., 2015) in order to see the frequencies of the syntactic relations; 2) the corpus *Zernola* (Gonzalez-Dios et al., 2014) to see if the syntactic relations are also used in simple texts; and 3) a lemma frequency list (Gonzalez-Dios, 2016) to see the frequencies of the discourse markers and lexical signals.

3 Framework for the Analysis of Simplified Texts

In this section, we present the framework and the annotation required to perform the analysis of simplified texts taking discourse into account.

3.1 Simplification Annotation and Analysis

Following Gonzalez-Dios et al. (2016), we propose to annotate whether the target clauses, in our case the causal relations, have been treated or not (binary tagging). If so, which operations have been performed in each structure. Besides, in this study, we add complementary descriptions such as clause length, syntactic depth (depth of the syntactic tree), surrounding phenomena or frequency information. These are the questions we propose:

a) Simplification treatment and macro-operations:
- Have the syntactic, DMs and lexical signals been treated or not? In the case of the syntactic signals, we also analyze if they have been treated or not according to the causal type defined by *Euskaltzaindia* (Euskaltzaindia, 2011): *i)* pure causal *-(e)lako* 'because', *ii)* causal explicative *bait-* 'since' and *iii)* pseudo-causal *-(e)nez* 'as').
- When the simplification is performed, we ask: which macro-operations have been performed? For each macro-operation, which exact operations? In the case of lexical signals, which operations according to the PoS (verbs or nouns)?

b) Length and depth
- The sentences that have been split are longer than the average sentence length of original clause?
- The sentences that have been split are inside another subordinate clause?

c) Frequencies
- In the case of the syntactic signals, are they also frequent in other corpora? For this analysis, the frequencies of other corpora are needed.
- When performing transformations, have the syntactic, DMs and lexical signals been substituted with a more frequent equivalent one?

d) Ordering
- In the case of the syntactic signals, do the reordering operations suit the word order found in other corpora or the canonical RST relation order?
- Do they suit canonical or stylistic word or sentence orders?

3.2 Discourse Annotation (RST) and Analysis

In the discourse analysis, we want to know if the relations found in the original texts have been kept, modified or deleted in the simplified texts. To that end, we follow this procedure:

- Segmentation: automatic fine-grained discourse segmentation with EusEduSeg (Iruskieta and Zapirain, 2015) and manually corrected following Iruskieta (2014). Output format: RS3.
- Rhetorical structure annotation: manually annotated with RSTTool (O'Donnell, 2000) following a modular and incremental annotation method (Pardo, 2005). Output format: RS3.
- Description if there were maintained or changed the nucleus-satellite order of the relations and the relation names with the Rhetorical DataBase (RhetDB) (Pardo, 2005).

In order to describe the simplification operations at rhetorical structure level, we propose the following questions:

a) Rhetorical relations:
- What kind of rhetorical relations were deleted from the original sentences in the intuitive corpus-set and in the structural corpus-set?

- Which relations have been added for text simplification?

b) Ordering:

- Has the nucleus-satellite order been maintained in rhetorical relations?[4]

3.3 Joint Annotation and Analysis

In order to join both analyses and based on the previous annotation, we propose to analyze the influence of simplification operations in discourse looking at the elementary discourse units (EDU), the central subconstituent (CSC)[5] and the rhetorical relations (RR). Exactly, we look the simplification operations performed which impact have on discourse. So, for each relation we make a description like the one that follows for the structurally simplified sentence presented in Table 1: *i*) an insert (*hegoaren formak* 'the shapes of the wings') has been performed in the clausal proposition; *ii*) two split and three insert operations (*izan ere, Hegoaren forma* 'due to the shape of the wings' and *ordea* 'however') in the surrounding phenomena.

Regarding rhetorical structure, we based on the simplification annotation and in the RST trees like the one presented in Figure 1, where the rhetorical structure (RS-tree) of the original text is shown above and the RS-tree of the structurally simplified text is bellow. There are three main changes in Figure 1: *i*) there is one span missing (4 above and 3 bellow), *ii*) the CAUSE relation is attached directly to the most important EDU of the RS-tree (to the central subconstituent), and *iii*) the CONCESSION relation has a new order (SN above and NS bellow) and is attached to a bigger text span (EDU_{1-2} bellow)[6].

In order to quantify and summarize that, these are the questions we propose:

a) Treatment in simplification:

- Has it been treated or not?

b) Elementary discourse unit (EDU):

---

[4]This is important as Mann and Thompson (1987) state: "if a natural text is rewritten to convert the instances of non-canonical span order to canonical order, it seldom reduces text quality and often improves it".

[5]The CSC is the salient EDU of a text span.

[6]Other changes were done in signaling the relations: in the signal CAUSE, the causal subordinator *-lako* 'since' was changed into the explicative connector *izan ere* 'since'.
And in the signal CONCESSION the subordinator *nahiz eta ...-n* 'in spite of' was changed into the connector *ordea* 'however'.

- Does the EDU number remain the same? If it changes, which are the changes?

c) Central subconstituent (CSC):

- Are there any changes in the CSC? Which?

d) Rhetorical relations (RR):

- Are the RRs kept? Which ones?
- Are there new RRs?
- Which RRs have been added, modified or deleted?

This way we see how the simplification operations affect discourse.

4 Results of the Quantitative Analysis

In this section, we present the results and analysis of the causal relations (our sample) according to the framework presented in Section 3.

4.1 Results of Simplification Analysis

Treatment and macro-operations: In Table 4 we present the results in relation to the treatment in both simplification approaches. As we can see: *i*) more syntactic signals have been treated in the intuitive approach; *ii*) results in the lexical signals are similar; *iii*) and discourse markers do not seem to be treated in any case.

Treated	Structural		Intuitive	
Syntactic	47.06	(8/17)	64.71	(11/17)
DMs	25.00	(4/16)	6.25	(1/16)
Lexical	21.21	(7/34)	24.24	(8/34)

Table 4: Percentages and raw numbers of causal relations

Focusing on the different types of causal syntactic signals (Table 5), we see that there is a tendency to treat the pure causal *-(e)lako* 'because' in the structural approach, while explicative *bait-* 'since' is treated in the intuitive approach.

	Structural		Intuitive	
Pure *-(e)lako*	55.56	(4/9)	33.33	(3/9)
Explicative *bait-*	40.00	(2/5)	100.00	(5/5)
Pseudo *-(e)nez*	33.33	(1/3)	100.00	(3/3)

Table 5: Treated Clauses according to the causal type in both approaches

Looking at the macro-operations (Table 6) we see that, in our sample, while the syntactic signals undergo split and transformation operations, the discourse markers

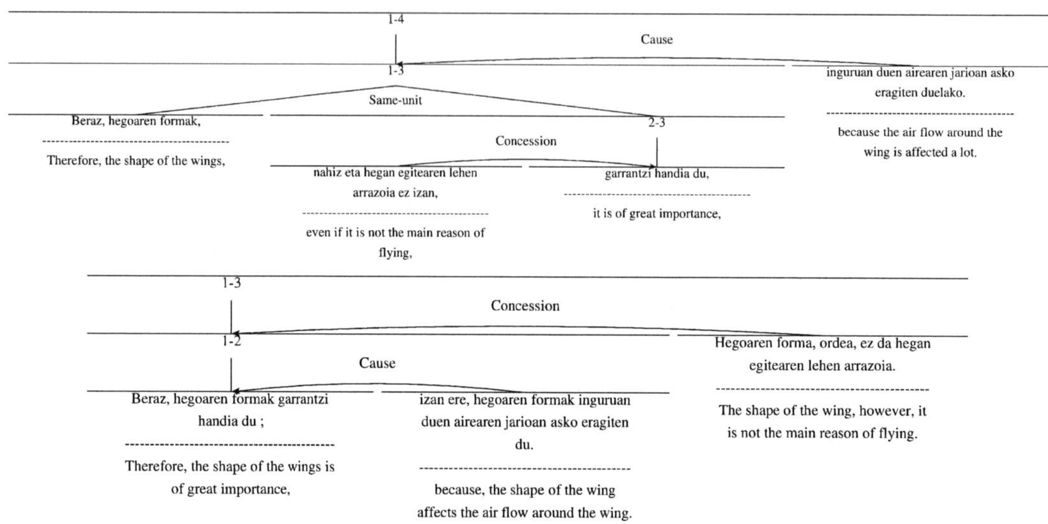

Figure 1: *Bernoulli_80* sentence's original (above) and structural (bellow) RS-trees

undergo transformations (as they are lexical units they cannot undergo splitting operations). The lexical signals undergo split and transformation operations in the structural approach, but only transformations in the intuitive.

Comparing the approaches, it is noticeable that more split operations are performed in the structural approach and more transformations in the intuitive. Exactly, the transformations performed in syntactic signals are: i) transforming a subordinate clause into a main clause ii) reformulations (more than one operations and paraphrases) and ii) changing the syntactic signal.

Regarding discourse markers, the transformation that has been performed is the substitution of a discourse marker for a more frequent one. The other macro-operations are delete and reordering.

In the case of the lexical signals, the operations performed vary according to the PoS. In Table 7 we present figures about the number of operations performed in nouns and verbs.

To summarize the analysis of the operations, we see that some macro-operations are restricted to the relation type and the PoS of it. That is, we see that no split is applied in all causal DMs or in all noun causal signals. For example, in the causal clause of sentence presented in Table 1, an insert has been performed in the structural approach; in the intuitive approach a split, a transformation (subordinate to main clause) and an insert have been performed.

Length and depth: The average length of the causal clauses in our original sample are 7 words[7]. In the intuitive approach, the split operations have been carried out in all the clauses with 7 or more words, but this only happens in 2 out of the 5 split operations carried out in the structural approach. In relation to the depth, two of the split operations in the structural approach were performed in subordinate clauses inside subordinate clauses e.g. a relative clause inside a noun clause.

Frequencies: Related to the description of the syntactic structures contained in the CBST, we have checked if they are also frequent structures in the BDT corpus[8] and in the *Zernola* corpus. As we can see, they are all frequent structures in both corpora (Table 8).

In Table 9 we present some transformation operations involving substitutions. Our analysis lead us to propose some preliminary conclusions: syntactic signals and DMs are not always substituted with more frequent equivalent ones, but with less ambiguous. As we see here, more frequent forms do not always mean simplicity.

Ordering: In relation to the reordering operations, we have analyzed whether the movements carried out

---

[7]As mentioned before, there are 17 clauses with syntactic relations. The longest of them has 17 words and the shortest 3. The mode is 4 words and the median 6.

[8]We consider a structure as frequent when it has more than 10 % of occurrences in its type.

| Macro-oper. | Only split | | Only trans | | Split+trans | | Only others | |
Approach	**Str.**	**Int.**	**Str.**	**Int.**	**Str.**	**Int.**	**Str.**	**Int.**
Syntactic	37.5	9.09	37.5	81.82	25.00	9.09	0.00	0.00
	(3/8)	(1/11)	(3/8)	(9/11)	(2/8)	(1/11)	(0/8)	(0/11)
DMs	0.00	0.00	25.00	100.00	0.00	0.00	75.00	0.00
	(0/4)	(0/1)	(1/4)	(1/1)	(0/4)	(0/1)	(3/4)	(0/1)
Lexical	42.86	0.00	42.86	50.00	0.00	0.00	14.29	50.00
	(3/7)	(0/8)	(3/7)	(4/8)	(0/7)	(0/8)	(1/7)	(4/8)

Table 6: Percentages and raw numbers of macro-operations performed in causal relations

| Oper. | Split | | Trans | | Reor. | | Delete | |
Appr.	**Str**	**Int**	**Str**	**Int**	**Str**	**Int**	**Str**	**Int**
Noun	0	0	1	3	1	1	0	1
Verb	3	0	2	1	0	0	0	2

Table 7: Macro-operations performed in the lexical signals according to their PoS

	BDT	Zernola
Pure *-lako*	26.91	28.10
Explicative *bait-*	39.94	46.28
Pseudo *-nez*	23.94	25.62
Others	9.21	0.00

Table 8: Distribution of causal structures in the corpora BDT and Zernola

in the simplified sentences at syntactic level suit the canonical word order or the order of clauses found in EPEC. In our sample no reordering was performed at that level. But, we did find an interesting reordering in the intuitive approach: a stylistic reordering took place in the signals in order to avoid the rear-burden [9]

4.2 Results of Discourse Analysis

In Table 10, we present the results obtained with Rhetorical Database in the different corpus-sets regarding simplification approaches and rhetorical relations. The number (K) of all the relations and the differences (diff.) of each corpus-set: *i)* relations of the original texts (source text) in the first two columns, *ii)* relations of the intuitively simplified texts in the following two, and *iii)* relations of the structurally simplified texts in the last two.

We can observe different simplification strategies in

Table 10:

— Less frequent RRs in both simplified datasets: the causal relation RESULT has less frequency in both simplified corpus-sets and CIRCUMSTANCE has also less frequency in both corpus-sets[10].

— More frequent RRs in both simplified datasets: SOLUTIONHOOD, CONCESSION and BACKGROUND are used to simplify texts.

— New RRs in one of the simplified datasets: PURPOSE, RESTATEMENT and MEANS are new relations in the intuitive approach and JOINT and PREPARATION in the structural.[11]

Using RhetDB, we extracted and presented in Table 11 the nuclearity type (SN: satellite first and nucleus after; NS: the other way around, nucleus first and satellite after) of all the hypotactic relations[12] and their frequencies.

Regarding Table 11, we see that the frequency of the causal relations (CAUSE, RESULT and PURPOSE) is bigger in the original subcorpus 0.411 (0.117 for SN and 0.294 for NS),[13] than in the intuitive 0.318 (SN: 0.09 and NS: 0.227) and structural approach 0.3 (SN: 0.00 and NS 0.3). This shows that there are less causal relations in the simplified datasets as also found by Graesser et al. (2004) and Crossley et al. (2012) and the NS order is preferred in the causal subgroup, when any causal relation is maintained.

Another interesting observation is that the NS ordering has been increased in the structural approach,

---

[9]"(...) "rear-burden" (...) [is] the effect that occurs when some key elements for correct processing of the message (e.g. the verb) are pushed towards the end of the sentence, thus delaying and making more difficult the comprehension of the message by the receiver." (Maia-Larretxea, 2015, 68).

[10]Although SAME-UNIT (SU) is not a relation, we report it, because it was also simplified in both corpus-sets.

[11]We think that RRs such as JOINT have appear because discourse was not taken into account when simplifying texts.

[12]Note that all multinuclear or paratactic relations were excluded from this analysis.

[13]The frequencies were normalized, as follows: original cause subgroup SN: the total K of the SN divided by the total K in the subcorpus: (2+1)/(9+8).

Type	Transformation	Explanation
Syntactic	*bait- -> -(e)lako*	causal explicative substituted with a pure causal (less frequent)
DMs	*horrez gain* 'moreover' -> *gainera* 'in addition'	substituted with a more frequent
	bada 'so', 'then', 'well' -> *hala ere* 'however'	substituted with a less frequent, but less ambiguous
Signals	*eragile* 'originator', 'promoter' -> *arrazoi* 'reason', 'cause', 'motive'	substituted with a more frequent near synonym

Table 9: Transformation operations involving substitutions

Source text Relations		Intuitive		Structural	
	K	**K**	**Diff.**	**K**	**Diff.**
Result	3	1	-2	2	-1
Circumstance	3	1	-2	1	-2
*Same-unit (SU)	4	3	-1	2	-2
Solutionhood	1	3	2	2	1
Concession	2	3	1	4	2
Background	1	2	1	2	1
Purpose	0	1	1	0	0
Restatement	0	1	1	0	0
Means	0	1	1	0	0
Preparation	0	0	0	1	1
Joint	0	0	0	1	1
Cause	3	4	1	3	0
Justify	1	1	0	1	0
Condition	1	2	1	1	0
No-conditional	1	1	0	1	0
Elaboration	1	1	0	0	-1
List	3	2	-1	4	1

Table 10: Simplification strategies and rhetorical relations

Relations	Original SN	Original NS	Intuitive SN	Intuitive NS	Structural SN	Structural NS
Cause	2	1	1	3		3
Justify		1		1		1
Result		3		1		2
Purpose			1			
Condition	1		1	1	1	
No-conditional	1		1		1	
Circumstance	1	2	1		1	
Solutionhood	1		3		1	1
Concession	2		3			2
Background	1		2			2
Restatement				1		
Means			1			
Preparation					1	
Elaboration		1		1		4
Total	9	8	14	8	5	15

Table 11: Nucleus/satellite ordering of the rhetorical relations in the original and simplified datasets

whereas in the intuitive approach the SN was increased (and, therefore, the NS decreased). This change brings the important message to the back of the structure and this way, it is more difficult to maintain all the information needed to understand the sentence in the memory, above all in the case of long sentences.

4.3 Joint Analysis

The results of the joint analysis of our sample are presented in Table 12. First column shows the sentence identifier, second column if it has been treated in simplification or nor, third column the changes performed in EDU frequency,[14] fourth column if the changes were

performed in the CSCs, the fifth column if RRs were maintained and the sixth column if RRs were changed.

To underline these results of Table 12 we summarized the most important differences in Table 13. We observe that the simplification operations performed in the intuitive (Int.) and structural (Str.) approaches are similar when simplifying (Simpl.), maintaining or changing the EDUs (Changes in EDUs), performing changes in the CSC and maintaining the RRs. But there is a great difference when they establish a new rhetorical relation (see Table 13), because there are only 3 changed relations (underlined in bold) in common: RESULT > CAUSE, CIRCUMSTANCE > CONDITION and +CONCESSION.

4.4 Concluding remarks

As a conclusion of this joint analysis, we think that rhetorical relations of the original texts were not always

---

[14]The sign '+' means that there are more EDUs or that some relation was added, whereas the sign '−' means that something is missing, for example '−info' means that there is less information. The sign > means that something at the left was changed by another thing to the right.

Text	Simpl.	Changes in EDUs	Changes in CSC	Maintained RRs	Changed RRs
Etxeko_19_int	YES			List	
Bernoulli_80_int	YES			Concession, Cause	
Exoplanetakv39_int	YES	+EDU		Cause	+Restatement
Exoplanetak33_int	NO			No-conditional	
Etxeko_20_int	NO	−Same-unit	−Same-unit, −info	Circumstance, Result	−Same-unit
Etxeko_28_int	YES			Justify	Result > Solutionhood
Exoplanetak_13_int	YES	+EDU		Condition, Elaboration	**Result** > **Cause**, +Solutionhood
Bernoulli_04_int	YES			Concession	**Circumstance** > **Condition**
Bernoulli_38_int	YES	+EDU	+EDU, −info	Background	+**Concession**
Etxeko_19_est	YES	+EDU	+EDU, −info	List	+Elaboration
Bernoulli_80_est	YES	−Same-unit	−Same-unit	Concession, Cause	−Same-unit
Exoplanetak_39_est	YES				Cause > Joint (NS > NN)
Exoplanetak_33_est	YES	+EDU	−Info	No-conditional, Same-unit	+Concession, +Preparation
Etxeko_20_est	YES		+N	Circumstance, Result	+Contrast
Etxeko_28_est	NO			Justify, Result	
Exoplanetak_13_est	YES			Condition, Elaboration	**Result** > **Cause**
Bernoulli_04_est	YES		CU changed	Concession	**Circumstance** > **Condition**
Bernoulli_38_est	YES	+EDU	+EDU, −info	Background	+**Concession**, +Solutionhood

Table 12: Contingency table of the joint analysis

	Simpl.	EDU	CSC	RR
Int.	7 Yes 2 No	3 +EDU 1 −SU	1 −SU −info 1 +EDU −info	12 kept 6 changed
Str.	8 Yes 1 No	3 +EDU 1 −SU	2 +EDU −info 1 −info 1 −SU 1 Change the CSC 1 NN	12 kept 9 changed 1 NS > NN

Table 13: Results of the joint analysis

taken into account when simplifying them (most of them were maintained). So, we want to propose for future simplification guidelines that not only lexis or syntax should be taken into account, but also discourse. That is, if in the original text there is a significant discourse relation, it should be kept in the simplified text when it helps comprehension but deleted when it leads to confusion. But the need of the discourse would not be limited to relations but to the overall relational discourse structure when simplifying text manually, the CSC and the same-unit should also be carefully treated.

For automatic texts simplification systems, the detection of the CSC should also be an important step, above all in the cases that the main piece of information should be highlighted. The difficult task of detecting the same-unit constructions could also be interesting, so that they should be deleted as much as possible.

5 Conclusion and Future Work

In this paper, we present a framework for the analysis of simplified texts taking discourse into account. In the simplification analysis, we propose to analyze the treatment and its the macro-operations, the length and depth, the frequencies and the reordering; in the discourse analysis, we propose to segment, annotate and describe the rhetorical relations; and, in the joint analysis, we propose to see the impact of simplification operations on the elementary discourse units, central subconstituents and rhetorical relations. Preliminary results show that this framework is useful to describe the simplified texts and that discourse is not always taken into account when simplifying texts in our datasets with the risk of creating not-coherent simplified texts. We have seen e.g. that some macro-operations such as the split cannot be applied to all the relations and that being more frequent does not involve simplicity as took for granted many times.

Currently, we are searching for more simplified texts in Basque to get more data and asking more people to simplify them, in order to get ride of the possible bias caused by the people who simplified the texts. Moreover, we are annotating in the Corpus of Basque Simplified Texts (CBST) more rhetorical relations to understand or describe all the simplification mechanisms. In the near future, we also want to perform this analysis with entire texts and not only sentences.

Acknowledgments

This study was carried out within the framework of the following projects: IXA group, Research Group (GIU16/16) and TUNER (TIN2015-65308-C5-1-R).

References

[Bott and Saggion2011] Stefan Bott and Horacio Saggion. 2011. An Unsupervised Alignment Algorithm for Text Simplification Corpus Construction. In *Proceedings of the Workshop on Monolingual Text-To-Text Generation*, MTTG '11, pages 20–26, Stroudsburg, PA, USA. Association for Computational Linguistics.

[Brunato et al.2015] Dominique Brunato, Felice Dell'Orletta, Giulia Venturi, and Simonetta Montemagni. 2015. Design and Annotation of the First Italian Corpus for Text Simplification. In *The 9th Linguistic Annotation Workshop held in conjuncion with NAACL 2015*, pages 31–41.

[Caseli et al.2009] Helena M. Caseli, Tiago F. Pereira, Lucia Specia, Thiago. A. S. Pardo, Caroline. Gasperin, and Sandra Aluísio. 2009. Building a Brazilian Portuguese Parallel Corpus of Original and Simplified Texts. In *the Proceedings of CICLing*, pages 59–70.

[Crossley et al.2007] Scott. A. Crossley, Max M. Louwerse, Philip M. McCarthy, and Danielle S. McNamara. 2007. A Linguistic Analysis of Simplified and Authentic Texts. *The Modern Language Journal*, 91(1):15–30.

[Crossley et al.2012] Scott A Crossley, David Allen, and Danielle S McNamara. 2012. Text Simplification and Comprehensible Input: A case for an Intuitive Approach. *Language Teaching Research*, 16(1):89–108.

[Euskaltzaindia2011] Euskaltzaindia. 2011. VII, (Perpaus jokatugabeak: denborazkoak, kausazkoak eta helburuzkoak, baldintzazkoak, kontzesiozkoak, moduzkoak, erlatiboak eta osagarriak) [VII (Subordinate Clauses-2, temporal, Causal and Purpose, Conditional, Concessive, Modal, Relative and Completive]. In *Euskal Gramatika Lehen Urratsak [Basque Grammar First Steps]*. Euskaltzaindia, Bilbo.

[Gonzalez-Dios et al.2014] Itziar Gonzalez-Dios, María Jesús Aranzabe, Arantza Díaz de Ilarraza, and Haritz Salaberri. 2014. Simple or Complex? Assessing the Readability of Basque Texts. In *Proceedings of COLING 2014, the 25th International Conference on Computational Linguistics: Technical Papers*, pages 334–344, Dublin, Ireland, August. Dublin City University and Association for Computational Linguistics.

[Gonzalez-Dios et al.2015] Itziar Gonzalez-Dios, María Jesús Aranzabe, and Arantza Díaz de Ilarraza. 2015. Perpaus adberbialen agerpena, maiztasuna eta kokapena EPEC-DEP corpusean [Presence, frequency and Position of Basque Adberbial Clauses in The BDT corpus]. Technical report, University of the Basque Country (UPV/EHU) UPV/EHU/LSI/TR 02-2015.

[Gonzalez-Dios et al.2016] Itziar Gonzalez-Dios, María Jesús Aranzabe, and Arantza Díaz de Ilarraza. 2016. A Preliminary Study of Statistically Predictive Syntactic Complexity Features and Manual Simplifications in Basque. In *Proceedings of the Computational Linguistics for Linguistic Complexity (CL4LC) workshop at Coling 2016*, pages 89–97.

[Gonzalez-Dios2016] Itziar Gonzalez-Dios. 2016. *Euskarazko egitura sintaktiko konplexuen analisirako eta testuen sinplifikazio automatikorako proposamena-Readability Assessment and Automatic Text Simplification. The Analysis of Basque Complex Structures*. Ph.D. thesis, University of the Basque Country (UPV/EHU).

[Graesser et al.2004] Arthur C. Graesser, Danielle S. McNamara, Max M. Louwerse, and Zhiqiang Cai. 2004. Coh-Metrix: Analysis of text on cohesion and language. *Behavior Research Methods*, 36(2):193–202.

[Iruskieta and Zapirain2015] Mikel Iruskieta and Benat Zapirain. 2015. Euseduseg: A Dependency-based EDU Segmentation for Basque. *Procesamiento del Lenguaje Natural*, 55:41–48.

[Iruskieta et al.2016] Mikel Iruskieta, María Jesús Aranzabe, Arantza Díaz de Ilarraza, and Mikel Lersundi. 2016. Kausazko koherentzia-erlazioen azterketa automatikoa euskarazko laburpen zientifikoetan [Toward a computational approach of causal coherence relations in scientific abstract texts]. *Gogoa*, 14:45–77.

[Iruskieta2014] Mikel Iruskieta. 2014. *Pragmatikako erlaziozko diskurtso-egitura: deskribapena eta bere ebaluazioa hizkuntzalaritza konputazionalean [The Discourse Structure of the Pragmatic Relations: Description and its Evaluation in Computational Lingustics]*. Ph.D. thesis, University of the Basque Country (UPV/EHU).

[Klaper et al.2013] David Klaper, Sarah Ebling, and Martin Volk. 2013. Building a German/Simple German Parallel Corpus for Automatic Text Simplification. In *Proceedings of the Second Workshop on Predicting and Improving Text Readability for Target Reader Populations*, pages 11–19, Sofia, Bulgaria, August. Association for Computational Linguistics.

[Klerke and Søgaard2012] Sigrid Klerke and Anders Søgaard. 2012. DSim, a Danish Parallel Corpus for Text Simplification. In Nicoletta Calzolari (Conference Chair), Khalid Choukri, Thierry Declerck, Mehmet Uğur Doğan, Bente Maegaard, Joseph Mariani, Jan Odijk, and Stelios Piperidis, editors, *Proceedings of the Eight International Conference on Language Resources and Evaluation (LREC'12)*, pages 4015–4018, Istanbul, Turkey, May. European Language Resources Association (ELRA).

[Kong et al.2017] Anthony Pak-Hin Kong, Anastasia Linnik, Sam-Po Law, and Waisa Wai-Man Shum. 2017. Measuring Discourse Coherence in Anomic Aphasia Using

Rhetorical Structure Theory. *International Journal of Speech-Language Pathology*, pages 1–16.

[Maia-Larretxea2015] Julian Maia-Larretxea. 2015. On Criteria of Professionals of the Language about the Back-burden in Basque. *Procedia-Social and Behavioral Sciences*, 212:67–73.

[Mann and Thompson1987] William C Mann and Sandra A Thompson. 1987. *Rhetorical structure theory: A theory of text organization*. University of Southern California, Information Sciences Institute.

[Mann and Thompson1988] William C. Mann and Sandra A. Thompson. 1988. Rhetorical Structure Theory: Toward a functional theory of text organization. *Text-Interdisciplinary Journal for the Study of Discourse*, 8(3):243–281.

[O'Donnell2000] Michael O'Donnell. 2000. RSTTool 2.4: a Markup Tool for Rhetorical Structure Theory. In *Proceedings of the first international conference on Natural language generation-Volume 14*, pages 253–256. Association for Computational Linguistics.

[Pardo2005] Thiago Alexandre Salgueiro Pardo. 2005. *Métodos para análise discursiva automática*. Ph.D. thesis, Instituto de Ciências Matemáticas e de Computação.

[Pellow and Eskenazi2014] David Pellow and Maxine Eskenazi. 2014. An Open Corpus of Everyday Documents for Simplification Tasks. In *Proceedings of the 3rd Workshop on Predicting and Improving Text Readability for Target Reader Populations (PITR)*, pages 84–93, Gothenburg, Sweden, April. Association for Computational Linguistics.

[Petersen and Ostendorf2007] Sarah E. Petersen and Mari Ostendorf. 2007. Text Simplification for Language Learners: A Corpus Analysis. In *In Proceedings of Workshop on Speech and Language Technology for Education. SLaTE*, pages 69–72. Citeseer.

[Saggion2017] Horacio Saggion. 2017. *Automatic Text Simplification*. Morgan & Claypool.

[Simensen1987] Aud Marit Simensen. 1987. Adapted Readers: How are they Adapted. *Reading in a Foreign Language*, 4(1):41–57.

[Xu et al.2015] Wei Xu, Chris Callison-Burch, and Courtney Napoles. 2015. Problems in Current Text Simplification Research: New Data Can Help. *Transactions of the Association for Computational Linguistics*, 3:283–297.

[Young1999] Dolly N. Young. 1999. Linguistic Simplification of SL Reading Material. Effective Instructional Practice? *The Modern Language Journal*, 83(3):350–366.

Using Rhetorical Structure Theory for

Detection of Fake Online Reviews

Olu Popoola, Aston University, UK.
essien.popoola@gmail.com

Abstract

Fake online book reviews, where authors and 'review factories' secretly pay writers to review products and services, are an increasing concern for consumer protection regulators worldwide. This study uses Rhetorical Structure Theory to analyze a forensic collection of authentic and fake Amazon book reviews drawn from a Deceptive Review corpus to test the potential for the application of discourse coherence analysis to the specific task of developing linguistic heuristics for spotting fake reviews and to the general area of linguistic deception detection. The study introduces a theory of genre violation to explain deception in reviews, highlights the deceptive pragmatics and discourse strategies of paid review writers and confirms the utility of RST in forensic linguistic contexts.

1   Introduction

Consumer protection laws and regulations in most 'free market' jurisdictions prohibit fake online reviews, undisclosed paid-for editorial content and misleading actions and omissions that (may) deceive the average consumer. Agents (i.e. paid writers) as well as businesses can be prosecuted. Since consumer education is key to fraud prevention, regulatory discourse routinely includes warnings and heuristics for detecting different kinds of fraud and deception. Many of these are based on noticing visual language features such as spelling mistakes and overly positive language that makes a product out to be 'the best thing ever' (Competition Bureau Canada, 2015).

The value and utility of these fake review detection heuristics could be improved by a systematic method of incorporating discourse-level features.

These may be easier to interpret and more amenable to regulatory heuristics development than stylometric measures (e.g. unigrams and syntax). This study deploys the analysis of discourse coherence relations to unlock linguistic information useful for heuristic development from within the structure, sequence and sections of a text.

Previous uses of RST for deception detection have had mixed results. Rubin et al. (2015) used RST to compare authentic news stories with fictional news stories written as competition entries for a 'Bluff the Listener' radio show. RST relations were found to have limited discriminatory power (63% accuracy), due to the latent influence of humour on linguistic profiles of both truths and lies. Feng (2015) tested an automated RST parser on a corpus of authentic TripAdvisor reviews and deceptive reviews written under experimental conditions. The parser underperformed (50% i.e. at chance level) compared to unigram (87%) and syntax (88%) measures; it was unable to identify a sufficiently diverse set of relations likely due to an absence of explicit discourse markers in the linguistic data which may be typical of product reviews.

This study addresses the limitations of this previous research. A manual RST analysis was conducted on a forensic corpus (i.e. real review data with established ground-truth) of 25 known fake and 25 authentic Amazon book reviews drawn from the Deceptive Review (DeRev) corpus (Fornaciari and Poesio, 2014). Previous deception detection research on this dataset has built machine learning models utilizing stylometric measures with relatively high accuracy levels of 75%-85% (Fornaciari   and   Poesio,   2014;   Hernández-

Proceedings of the 6th Workshop Recent Advances in RST and Related Formalisms, pages 58–63,
Santiago de Compostela, Spain, September 4 2017. ©2017 Association for Computational Linguistics

Castaneda et al, 2016); this study hypothesized that those observed stylometric differences reviews would manifest as significant variation in the coherence relational structure of fake compared to authentic reviews and qualitative differences in the pragmatic strategies of fake and true review writers.

2 Method and Data

The DeRev corpus is a collection of 6,819 Amazon book reviews of 68 books written by 4811 different reviewers. This study focused on the 118 'gold standard' fake reviews. Ground-truth for these fake reviews was obtained through following up the journalistic research of David Streitfield, who interviewed review writers that admitted to being paid $10 to $15 dollars per review ('offending writers'), 'offending authors' who admitted paying for bulk reviews (e.g. $999 for 50 reviews) and the owner of a review production factory who had been making over $20000 per month before being exposed (Streitfield, 2012).

Fornaciari and Poesio used Streitfield's investigative journalism to collect known fake reviews by searching Amazon for 1) reviews of books written by 'offending authors', and 2) reviews written by 'offending writers'. From those collected reviews, only those that matched the following set of meta-linguistic deceptive review heuristics were selected: a) be part of a review cluster i.e. one of at least two reviews posted for the same book within 72 hours. b) be written by an author that used a nickname rather than real name, and c): be assigned an 'Unknown' rather than Verified Amazon purchase status. The gold-standard corpus was completed with a matching number of reviews whose authenticity was established by the fact that the books authors were either dead (e.g. Ernest Hemmingway) or highly successful (e.g. Stephen King), making 236 reviews in total.

Manual RST coding was conducted by the author on 50 gold-standard reviews (25 true, 25 fake) all between 50 and 250 words in length (see Figure 1 above). Controlling for length minimized the effect of this variable on predicting deception with RST; this length was chosen as convenient and sufficient for manual RST coding.

DeRev-RST Corpus (Popoola, 2016)

	All reviews (50)	True (25)	Fake (25)
No. Words	4931	2222	2709
Average number of words per review / stdev	98.6 / 40.7	88.9 / 43.2	108.4 / 36.3
No. of RST coherence relations annotated	490	239	251
Average number of relations per review / stdev	9.8/5.0	9.6 / 5.6	10.0 / 4.4
Average 'words per relation' / stdev	10.7 / 2.6	10.0 / 2.9	11.3 / 2.1

Figure 1: DeRev-RST corpus statistics.

Macro-relation	RST relations	Macro-relation	RST relations
ATTRIBUTE	Attribute	EVALUATION	Comment
BACKGROUND	Background		Conclusion
	Circumstance		Evaluation
CAUSE	Cause	EXPLANATION	Justify
	Consequence		Reason
	Result		Evidence
COMPARISON	Analogy	JOINT	Disjunction
	Comparison		Joint
	Preference		List
CONTRAST	Antithesis	MANNER-MEANS	Manner
	Concession		Means
	Contrast	SUMMARY	Summary
ELABORATION	Elaboration		Restatement
ENABLEMENT	Enablement	TEMPORAL	Sequence
	Purpose		Temporal

Figure 2: RST macro-relations used and their definitions.

Carlson and Marcu's (2001) extended set of RST relations was used for initial coding but only the macro-relations (summary groupings of relations; see Figure 2 above) were used in the predictive analysis model to minimize the impact of ambiguous relations on coding consistency. Additionally, an external party collated the 50 reviews according to the sample specification (and renamed the files) so that the author could code the reviews blind to truth value.

3 Results

In the analysis of the corpus, the fake reviews have more *Elaboration, Joint* and *Background* macro-relations; the true reviews have more *Evaluation, Contrast and Explanation* macro-relations. Only True reviews contain *Comparison* relations.

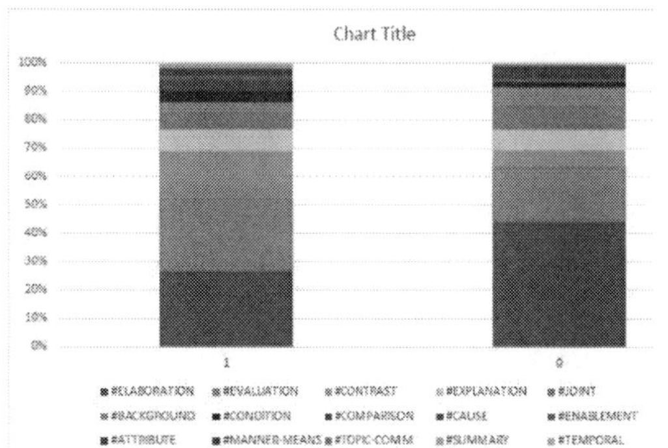

Figure 3: Comparative frequency of RST macro-relations. 1=True reviews (239 relations); 0=Fake reviews (251 relations)

The boxplots below (Figures 4 and 5) suggest that the use of *Elaboration* relation distinguishes true from fake reviews discourse. Although overall use of *Evaluation* macro-relations does not substantially differ between true and fake reviews, the relative proportion of *Evaluation* vs. *Elaboration* is much lower in deceptive reviews.

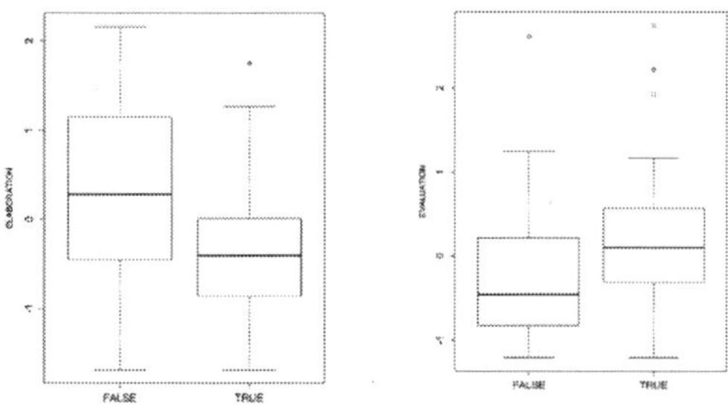

Figure 4: Boxplot comparison of Elaboration and Evaluation macro-relation frequencies in fake and true reviews.

The range of relation frequencies indicate significant effects for *Contrast* relations as a feature of authentic reviews. Specifically, 14 *Contrast_Concession* relations were only found in the true sample. 31 out of 37 *Contrast_Antithesis* relations were found in the true sample. Both authentic and deceptive reviews contain *Background* relations, although fake reviews use them more frequently. A logistic regression model that fit all 12 macro-relations (*R square = 0.68*) indicates that the differences for *Elaboration and Contrast* are significant (Figure 5a.)

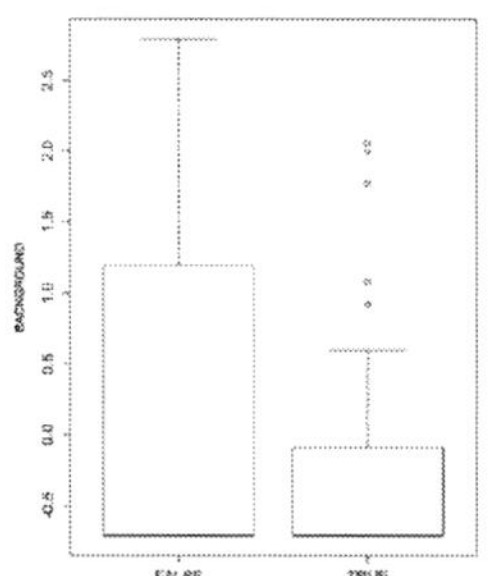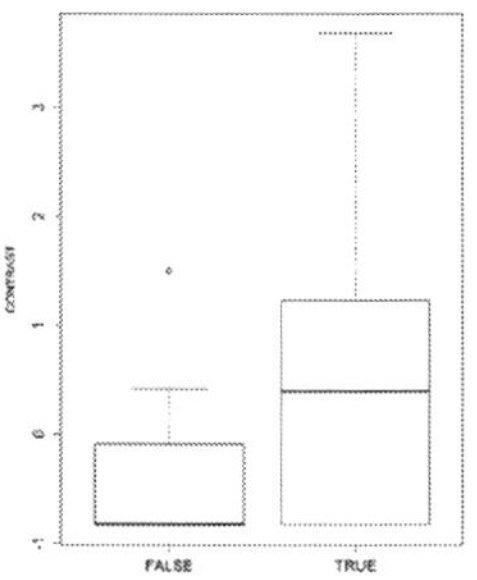

Figure 5: Boxplot comparison of Contrast and Background macro-relation frequencies in fake and true reviews

LOGISTIC REGRESSION

Relations (Total)	P score	Exp(B)
Contrast (86)	.02	.11
Elaboration (263)	.05	3.79
Background (38)	.17	2.08
Joint (54)	.23	2.32
Explanation (56)	.60	1.44
Evaluation (174)	.67	.77

Hosmer+Lemshow = 0.77; Nagelkerke R Square=0.68]

Figure 5a: Logistic regression results for six most frequent relations in DeRev-RST corpus.

4 Discussion

4.1 Elaboration

While the high frequency of *Elaboration* relations is generally to be expected in RST analysis, the fact that paid-for reviews use significantly more *Elaboration* relations than authentic ones reflects the deceptive context of communication. In fake reviews, there is more synopsis and description of topics; the plot elaboration in Figure 6 takes up half of the total review. This is likely due to paid review writers, who at most only superficially read the books they are reviewing, using information that is easily gleaned from book PR materials e.g. back cover synopsis.

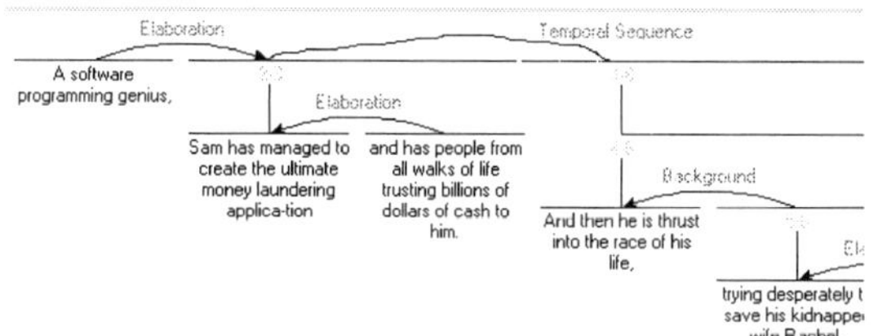

Figure 6: Plot elaboration in a fake review

Being paid £5 to £10 per review means that for the activity to be profitable, time must be spent on writing multiple reviews rather than reading many books. This inevitably affects the quality of evaluation and appraisal of the books.

4.2 Evaluation

While the frequency of *Evaluation* relations does not clearly discriminate between fake and authentic reviews, a lower proportion of evaluative text is a feature of the deceptive reviews; where true reviews have on average equal amounts *Elaboration and Evaluation*, fake reviews have a 2:1 ration (see Figure 4 above). Paid writers often use generic appraisal, simply adding phrases such as *"...a must read..."* or *"I would recommend..."* to the end of a descriptive review. In contrast, *Evaluation* in the genuine reviews is longer and more subjective i.e. explaining why the reviewer liked the book rather than why the reader would like the book.

FAKE: This is a must read for anyone considering taking the Hobet examination and is looking for a sure-fire way to succeed.

TRUE: This book made me think and made me remember that it is okay to dream. Who can argue with that?

Figure 7: Comparative examples of *Evaluation*

4.3 Contrast

A significant feature of authentic reviews was the use of *Contrast* relations with an evaluative function. The true reviews are far more likely to mention potentially negative aspects of a book in the context of an overall positive appraisal; *Contrast* relations (which include *Concession* and *Antithesis*) are the discourse mechanism for this (e.g. Fig 8 below).

This strategy of expressing 'caveats' has been noted as a feature of negative English language movie reviews (Taboada et al, 2014). Hedged positive evaluation has also been found to feature in Japanese academic book reviews (Itakura, 2013). Mitigated evaluation is a feature of the review genre (at least in certain languages/cultures).

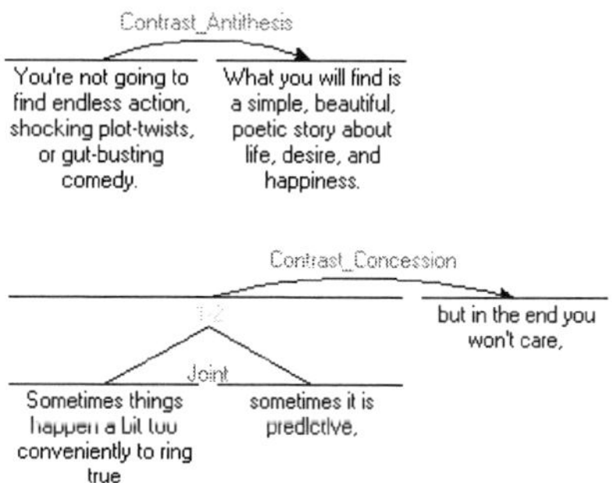

Figure 8: Examples of *Contrast* relations in true reviews.

This sets up the hypothesis that deceptive reviews are a *genre (or register) violation*. The situational context of the deception – individuals producing multiple reviews, under time constraints that prohibit proper reading, to maximize income – impacts on the pragmatic and discourse strategies of paid writers and affect the language choices made. Under these conditions providing the nuanced opinion typical of the review genre is both challenging and inefficient.

4.4 *Background*

The *Background* relation did not show a significant effect (see Figures 5 and 5a above) but its use in fake reviews present examples of *deceptive pragmatics*. Deceptive use of *Background* relations deploys persuasion to affect reader perceptions of the review rather than of the book – as if the reader needs convincing of the veracity of the review. One example,
in Figure 9 below, has a *Background* relation with a *Reason* relation in the satellite presenting a motivation for purchase.

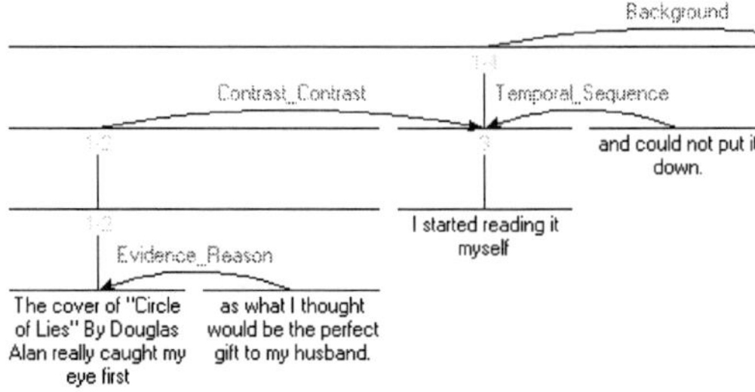

Figure 9: Examples of *Background* in a fake review.

4.5 *Nuclearity*

The qualitative content and location of the "most nuclear" discourse unit (Stede, 2008) is a predictor of deception in these reviews. Mann and Thompson's (1987) deletion test and Marcu's (2000) Strong Nuclearity Hypothesis were used to locate the 'nucleus discourse unit'(NDU) for each review.

	Fake (25)	True (25)
NDU in 1st sentence of review	17	9
NDU mentions *Title*	18	3
NDU mentions *Author*	8	5
NDU describes content/plot	8	4
NDU contains appraisal/evaluation	18	22

Figure 10: Comparative analysis of NDUs

Figure 10 illustrates marked differences in the NDUs of the fake and real reviews. The fake review NDUs were mainly located in the opening sentence, typically mentioned the book title and often provided author name with a brief plot/content description (e.g. Fig 11 below). Authentic review NDUs contained a key evaluation/opinion of the book without (or with minimal) content or plot description and were more likely to occur within the body of the review (e.g. Fig 12 below).

This unexpected finding suggests that techniques for identifying salient discourse such as automatic summarization may be useful for computer-aided deception detection and further supports the use of RST and related formalisms in the development of a linguistic theory of deception.

5. Conclusion

This pilot study has revealed that paid review writers deploy deceptive pragmatics i.e. a coherent set of linguistic strategies deployed to support the intent to deceive. Deceptive reviews contain violations of genre conventions related to evaluation, and contamination from related genres such as synopsis or press release. RST analysis has provided rich qualitative data for the generation of a set of regulatory heuristics that might include consumer warnings such as: 1) fake reviews are *more* likely to mention book titles, authors and give details of a book's contents; 2) fake 5-star reviews tend to be all positive, whereas genuine 5-star reviews usually contain caveats. Future research will address the challenge of replicating RST analysis on big linguistic data sets by identifying relations signals to assist automated analysis, testing the potential of 'textual coherence ratios' such as *Elaboration/Evaluation* as explanatory 'discourse metrics' and investigating whether models of discourse salience and summarization tool can be used in deception detection.

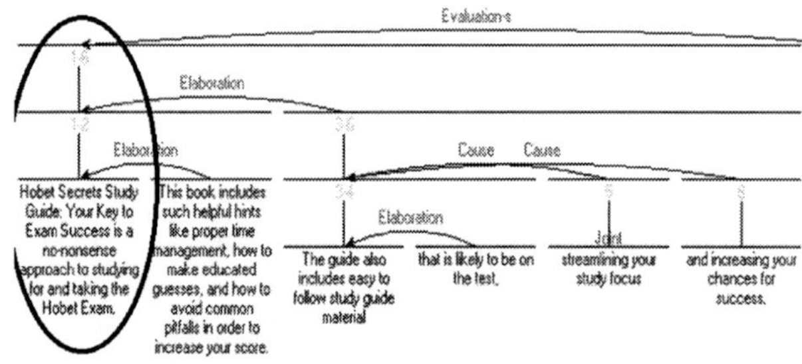

Figure 11: Fake review NDU located in opening sentence.

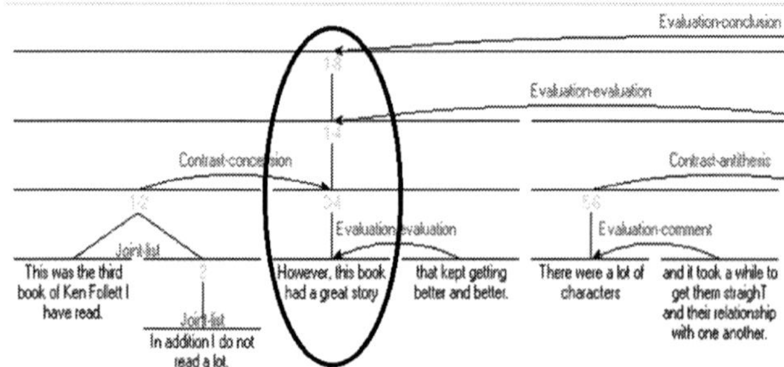

Figure 12: True review NDU located in body of text.

References

Carlson, Lynn., and Marcu, Daniel (2001) *Discourse tagging reference manual.* ISI Technical Report ISI-TR-545, 54, 56

Competition Bureau Canada (2015) *Don't buy into fake online endorsements.* Retrieved from http://www.competitionbureau.gc.ca/eic/site/cb-bc.nsf/eng/03782.html

Feng, Vanessa W. (2015) *RST-style discourse parsing and its applications in discourse analysis.* Doctoral Dissertation, University of Toronto.

Fornaciari, Tommaso, Poesio, Massimo. (2014). *Identifying fake Amazon reviews as learning from crowds.* Proceedings of the 14th Conference of the European Chapter of the Association for Computational Linguistics, pages 279–287

Itakura, Hiroko. (2013). *Hedging praise in English and Japanese book reviews.* Journal of Pragmatics, 45(1), 131-148.

Mann, William C., and Christian MIM Matthiessen. "Functions of language in two frameworks." *Word* 42, no. 3 (1991): 231-249.

Mann, William C., and Sandra A. Thompson. *Rhetorical structure theory: A theory of text organization.* University of Southern California, Information Sciences Institute, 1987.

Marcu, Daniel. *The theory and practice of discourse parsing and summarization.* MIT press, 2000.

Rubin, Victoria L., Conroy, Niall J., and Chen, Yimin. (2015) *Towards news Verification: Deception detection methods for news discourse.* In Proceedings of HICSS48 Symposium on Rapid Screening Technologies, Deception Detection and Credibility Assessment Symposium

Stede, Manfred. "RST revisited: Disentangling nuclearity." *Subordination 'versus' Coordination 'in Sentence and Text* (2008): 33-59.

Streitfield, David (2012) *The best book reviews money can buy.* Retrieved from http://www.nytimes.com/2012/08/26/business/book-reviewers-for-hire-meet-a-demand-for-online-raves.html

Taboada, Maite, Carretero, Marta and Hinnell, Jennifer (2014) *Loving and hating the movies in English, German and Spanish.* Languages in Contrast, 14(1), 127-161.

"Haters gonna hate": challenges for sentiment analysis of Facebook comments in Brazilian Portuguese

Juliano Desiderato Antonio
Universidade Estadual de Maringá
jdantonio@uem.br

Ana Carolina Leatte Santin
Universidade Estadual de Maringá
leattesantin@gmail.com

Abstract

The aim of this paper is to present reflections from Discourse Analysis and from Construction Grammar on the creation of a dictionary for sentiment analysis of Facebook comments. The reflections from Discourse Analysis address problems such as the identification of the semantic orientation of words that present opposite polarities depending on the ideological formation of the speaker. Another reflection from Discourse Analysis regards the fact that the writers of the comments use nouns and noun phrases not only to name some entity, but also to build discourse objects in a way that the label they give to the discourse objects reveals an evaluation. In order to analyze constructions larger than words, such as idioms, we draw on Construction Grammar principles. The investigation of constructions and idioms can provide a better understanding of sentiment in text. The *corpus* consists of comments extracted manually from Facebook public discussion pages related to diverse themes, such as politics, education, religion, music, lifestyle etc.

1 Introduction

Facebook is one of the websites with higher data traffic on the internet. On December 2016 it registered 1.86 billion monthly active users (nearly 1 in 4 people worldwide). In Brazil, the ratio is even higher: nearly 55.5% of the population were active Facebook users in November 2016 (Facebook, 2017). Thus, linguists who are interested in investigating language in use have on Facebook an immeasurable research field.

Wilson et al.'s (2012) comprehensive review about scientific research conducted about Face-book in the social sciences points to the need for social engagement as the main motivation for people to use Facebook. Seidman (2014) investigated the expression of the "true self" on Facebook, which "consists of qualities that an individual currently possesses but does not normally express to others in everyday life". The need for social engagement and the expression of the true self are encompassed within the metafunctions[1] proposed by Halliday (1985). The ideational metafunction regards self-expression, as it concerns the grammatical features used to construct both the speaker's inner experiences and the experiences with the world around him. On the other hand, the interpersonal metafunction is related to the grammatical resources used by the speaker to interact with his/her interlocutors, assuming social roles and roles concerning the communicative situation (social engagement). Whilst the ideational and the interpersonal are extralinguistic metafunctions, the textual metafunction deals with the presentation of interpersonal and ideational content in the form of information that can be shared by the speaker and his / her interlocutors by means of texts. In other words, texts produced by Facebook users and their linguistic behavior deserve being studied by linguists.

According to Iruskieta et al. (2013), Computational Linguistics depends on discourse annotated *corpora* for the creation of automatic applications. The research that resulted in this paper intends to create a dictionary for sentiment analysis by extracting comments from Facebook public pages related to diverse themes, such as politics, education, religion, music, lifestyle etc.

---

[1] "Metafunction refers to the different modes of meaning construed by the grammar."

Proceedings of the 6th Workshop Recent Advances in RST and Related Formalisms, pages 64–72,
Santiago de Compostela, Spain, September 4 2017. ©2017 Association for Computational Linguistics

However, as we started analyzing the semantic orientation of the comments, we noticed that the same words said by different people had polar opposite semantic orientation, as in examples (1) and (2).

(1) Só come "pala" da *Direita* quem for analfabeto político e funcional.

Only functional and political illiterate people believe in the lies of the *right wing*.

(2) ... nós da *Direita* não temos político de estimação.

We, who are *right wing*, do not have pet politicians.

In (1) "right wing" is considered negative by the writer of the comment, as it can be presupposed that assumptions endorsed by right wing are lies. On the other hand, in (2) the writer of the comment, who assumes to have a right wing political orientation, suggests that left wing people have pet politicians, whilst right wing people do not. Therefore, in (2), "right wing" is evaluated positively. That happens because the comments collected were produced by people with different views on the issues discussed in the pages and we decided to draw attention to such problem, as it certainly creates difficulties for sentiment analysis.

Thus, this paper presents some challenges for the creation of a dictionary for sentiments analysis of Facebook comments in Brazilian Portuguese caused by the different positions assumed by the producers of the comments. Furthermore, it is also a goal of the paper to analyze other forms rather than nouns, adjectives, verbs, NPs. The investigation of constructions and idioms can provide a better understanding of sentiment in text.

In terms of structure, besides the introduction, this paper is divided in 4 more sections. In Section 2 we present a short view of what has been done about sentiment analysis in Linguistics and in NLP. We also introduce in Section 2 some theoretical assumptions from Discourse Analysis in order to face the challenges which are addressed in the paper. A brief review of Constructional Grammar is also presented in Section 2. In Section 3 we present the methodology used in the research and the discussion of the data is provided in Section 4. The last section of the paper is the Conclusion, followed by the references.

2 Theoretical background

In this section we provide a general background about what has been done regarding sentiment analysis and also some contributions from Discourse Analysis which are essential for the challenges discussed in the paper. A brief review of basic assumptions of Constructional Grammar is presented in order to provide a better understanding of the concepts of "construction" and "idiom".

2.1 Sentiment analysis

According to Taboada (2016), "sentiment analysis is a growing field at the intersection of linguistics and computer science that attempts to automatically determine the sentiment contained in text". Sentiment is conceived as positive or negative evaluation conveyed by linguistic expression, both lexical and grammatical. Beyond defining sentiment analysis, Taboada (2016) also presents a broad view of the contributions of Linguistics to automatic sentiment analysis.

Two main approaches are used for automatic extraction of sentiments: machine learning and lexicon based (Taboada, 2016). We will focus on the latter, as it is the type of method we intend to implement in the subsequent stages of the project we are developing.

Among the lexicon based approaches, Taboada (2016) mentions some dictionaries for sentiment analysis: SentiWordNet (Baccianella et al., 2010) catalogues about 38,000 words regarding their polarity; also based on polarity, Macquarie Semantic Orientation Lexicon (Mohammad et al., 2009) classifies almost 76,000 words; Subjectivity dictionary (Wilson et al., 2009) not only presents the polarity of the words, but also groups them according to their strength (strong positive, weak positive, neutral, weak negative, strong negative); Semantic Orientation Calculator (SO-CAL) (Taboada et al., 2011) stratifies about 5,000 words in a 10-point scale which ranges from -5 to +5.

In Brazilian Portuguese, among many works that deal with sentiment analysis, Sentimeter-Br (Rosa, 2015) is a mechanism for calculating semantic orientation. It is based on a dictionary of words divided according to the area they belong to, e.g. music, technology, beauty, business. The system also implements a mechanism (Enhanced Sentimeter) which uses the user's profile of a social media to calculate sentiment.

2.2 Contributions from Discourse Analysis

Regarding the problem presented in the introduction of the paper with the different evaluations of "right wing" held by the writers of the comments, which have opposite political views, Pêcheux (1975) states that words, expressions, propositions etc do not have a self-contained meaning. On the contrary, their meanings change according to the positions supported by the speakers who use them, i.e, their ideological formations. In (1) "right wing" has a negative evaluation because the comment was written by a person of left wing ideological formation. On the other hand, in (2) "right wing" has a positive evaluation because the writer of the comment belongs to a right wing ideological formation. Thus, ideological formation is an important feature to be taken into account in order to identify sentiment towards propositions.

Another important reflection from Discourse Analysis regards the difference between reference and *référenciation*[2] proposed by Mondada and Dubois (1995). When one makes reference, he / she names in an objective way anything that is in the world (*designatum*, according to Lyons [1977]). On the other hand, in the *référenciation* process, the speaker builds discourse objects in a way that they can be categorized and recategorized. In (3) the writer of the comment, which was taken from a left wing Facebook page, uses the "communist doctrinators" NP in order to show how a group of right wing people refers to teachers. Obviously, it is not only naming. If it were like this, the group which is criticized in the comment would use the noun "teachers". Actually, the "communist doctrinators" NP reveals the treatment of the right wing group towards the discourse object "teachers". External world class "teachers" is not affected by the way the right wing group refers to it, as "communist doctrinators" is a discourse object.

---

[2] We will use the French word "référenciation" (as Mondada and Dubois 1995) because there is not such word in English.

(3) Por isso mesmo, para isso funcionar, é preciso demonizar a classe dos professores como "*doutrinadores comunistas*", isto é, duas palavras que a direita adora usar.

For this reason, for this to work, it is necessary to demonize the class of the teachers as "communist doctrinators", i.e., two words that right wing loves to use.

In other words, in the view of *référenciation*, nouns and noun phrases do not only name a *designatum*, they also present an evaluation of the discourse object.

2.3 Constructions and idioms

Beyond nouns, adjectives, verbs, NPs, other forms should be investigated for a better understanding of sentiment in text. Constructions and idioms are widely used by speakers not only in face to face interactions, but also on social media.

According to Traugott and Trousdale (2013), constructions are form-meaning pairings and include morphemes, words, idioms, and abstract phrasal patterns (Goldberg, 2013; Hoffmann and Trousdale, 2013).

The term "construction grammar" (CG henceforth) refers to a group of distinct frameworks which share some tenets, summarized by Goldberg (2013) as follows:

i. Constructions are the basic units of grammar;

ii. Semantic structure is associated directly with syntactic structure without transformations or derivations;

iii. Constructions form a network in which nodes are related by inheritance links;

iv. Cross-linguistic variation can be explained in terms of domain-general cognitive processes or by the functions of the constructions involved;

v. Items and generalizations are part of the knowledge of language (this last tenet is shared by most, but not all approaches).

Formal classes	N
Nouns	136
Adjectives	156
Verbs	117
Constructions	22
Idioms	28

Table 1: Quantity of items per class.

Unlike Generative Grammar, CG considers grammar in a holistic way, i.e., no grammatical level is considered core or autonomous; a construction is formed by simultaneous work of phonology, morphosyntax, semantics and pragmatics (Traugott and Trousdale, 2013).

3 Methodology

The first step of the Methodology was to collect comments from public Facebook pages which discuss issues such as politics, education, religion, music, lifestyle etc. Nearly 1,000 comments were collected, segmented into EDUs[3] and classified either as subjective (present an evaluation) or objective (do not present an evaluation). The latter were eliminated from the corpus.

The remaining 649 EDUs were classified manually by two annotators as positive, negative or neutral, regarding the evaluation of a discourse object. The words and expressions responsible for the evaluation were extracted manually and divided according to their formal classes.

In Table 1 we present the quantity of words per class. Other features such as intensifiers, adverbs, interjections, signals of irony, laughing etc were also annotated but will not be discussed here as they do not refer directly to the main issue discussed in this paper. It is important to remark that words were counted only once, even if they were used more times in the *corpus*. Thus, the quantity in Table 1 refers to the quantity of words found and not to the amount of times they were used.

---

[3] "minimal building blocks of a discourse tree" (Carlson and Marcu, 2001). In general, EDUs are paratactic or hypotactic clauses, but not restrictive of completive clauses.

4 Discussion and analysis

In order to stress the importance of taking constructions into account in sentiment analysis, this Section is divided in two subsections: one for commonly investigated classes and forms such as nouns, adjectives, verbs, NPs, and one for constructions and idioms.

4.1 Nouns, adjectives, NPs, verbs

Within the view of *référenciation*, the speaker's communicative intentions govern his / her linguistic choices (Koch, 2002; 2007), as in example (4).

(4) Escola é um *depósito de criança*, APENAS, no fundo ninguém tá nem aí pro que é ensinado, só se interessam em ter um lugar pra deixar os "*presentes de Deus*" enquanto estão trabalhando. Por isso que quando tem greve os pais ficam tão irados.

School is a *children warehouse*, ONLY, actually nobody cares about what is taught, they are only interested in having a place to leave "*God's gifts*" while they are working. That's why parents get so mad when there is a teacher's strike.

In example (4) the writer of the comment quotes the opinion of people in general about Brazilian public schools, which are considered "depósito de criança" ("children warehouse"), i.e., a place where people leave their kids when they go to work. NP "depósito de criança" creates a discourse object which reveals a general conception about the *designatum* school.

Although NP "presentes de Deus" ("God's gifts") carries nouns of positive semantic orientation, it is written between "quotation marks", in a sarcastic way, which results in a negative evaluation of that discourse object. In other words, the writer of the comment means that there are moments when children are a nuisance to parents, who are not interested in their education, but only in having a place to leave them while they are at work.

Depreciatory collective nouns reveal the speaker's negative evaluation of a discourse object, especially when the referent is human (Neves, 2000). It is the case of the noun "bando" (which could be roughly translated into English as "gang"). In example (5), scoping adjective "demente" ("demented, in English), it evaluates negatively a group of people. In example (6), it is used to convey negative evaluation of a group of "machos" ("chauvinists", in English), which are also strongly qualified in a negative manner as "asquerosos" ("loathful").

(5) É só o reflexo de como viramos um *bando de dementes*.

It is only the reflex of how we became a *gang of demented*.

(6) *Bando de macho* asqueroso!

Gang of loathful *chauvinists*!

However, negative characteristics may be assumed by a group and transformed into positive evaluation. That's what happens with the expression "gang of crazy people"[4], in example (7), used by the supporters of Brazilian football team Sport Club Corinthians as a motivation yell.

(7) Aqui tem um *bando de loucos*, loucos por ti, Corinthians.

Here there is a *gang of crazy people*, crazy for you, Corinthians.

The comparison between examples (5) and (7) shows similarities – both NPs have the noun "gang" scoping an adjective from insanity semantic field – and also differences – in example (5) the evaluation is negative, while, in example (7), the evaluation is positive. To explain the differences, we have to cite Pêcheux (1975) again, to whom the meanings of words change according to the positions supported by the speakers who use them.

Nouns may lose their referential function in order to express quality (Neves, 2000) and, in such use, they can convey negative or positive evaluation. In example (8), noun "massa" ("mass") is not used to refer to "matter with no definite shape", but to qualify noun "página" ("page") as "cool".

(8) Aparece uma página que parece ser *massa*.

A page that seems to be *cool* shows up.

The same happens to noun "show" in example (9). Instead of naming a spectacle, it classifies the "debate" as "amazing, spectacular".

(9) O debate foi *show*.

The debate was *amazing*.

In example (10) noun "shit" qualifies noun "time" ("team") in an extremely pejorative way. In examples (11) and (12), besides the the change of position in the NP, the negative evaluation assigned to noun "filme" ("film") remains the same[5]. The possibility of such positional change is a particular characteristic of the grammar of Brazilian Portuguese. As it can be noticed, the translation into English is not even possible.

(10) Que time *merda*.

*What a *shit* team.

(11) *Merda* de filme.

Shit of film. (The appropriate translation would be "shitty film".)

(12) Filme *de merda*.

*Film of *shit*. (The appropriate translation would be "shitty film".)

Adjectives have been widely investigated in sentiment analysis due to their nature. According to Taboada (2016), "adjectives convey much of the subjective content in a text". However, not all adjectives can be used to evaluate. Classifier adjectives only subcategorize the nouns that they modify (Neves, 2000). As a result, they are not suitable for subjective evaluation, as in example (13), in which adjective "sexual" only specifies the type of

---

[4] In Brazilian Portuguese, the NP "bando de loucos" ("gang of crazy people") does not have the noun "people", as the adjective "crazy" can be used as a noun. Roughly, the literal translation would be "gang of crazies".

[5] In examples (10), (11) and (12), the correct translation would be "shitty". As in Brazilian Portuguese the noun "merda" ("shit") functions as an adjective, the same construction in English is ungrammatical.

"option" ("opção") mentioned by the writer of the comment.

(13) O que que a gente tem a ver com a opção *sexual* do outro?

What do we have to do with other people's sexual options?

On the other hand, qualifier adjectives, in a predication process, attribute properties to the nouns they modify. In example (14), the adjective assigns the quality "feliz" ("happy") to anyone who fulfills the conditions presented in the subject clause.

(14) *Feliz* é aquele que encontra a felicidade nos pequenos gestos.

Happy is the one who finds happiness in the small gestures.

Regarding syntactic use, adjectives can be predicative, as in example (15), in which "feio" ("ugly") is the nucleus of the VP, or adnominals, as in example (16), in which "louca" ("crazy"), "desequilibrada" ("unbalanced") and "insuportável" ("unbearable") modify noun "gente" ("people") within the NP.

(15) … se vier me perguntar se tu é feio…

… if you ask us if you are ugly…

(16) … gente muito louca, desequilibrada e insuportável…

… very crazy, unbalanced and unbearable people…

The semantic orientation of the NP is usually given by the adjective. In example (17), adjective "maravilhoso" ("wonderful") is responsible for the positive semantic orientation of the NP, whilst in example (18) adjective "fake" is responsible for the negative semantic orientation of the NP.

(17) Bar maravilhoso

Wonderful pub

(18) Sorriso falso

Fake smile

Verbs occupy the central role of a predication (Ilari and Basso, 2008). Thus, the correct identification of the semantic orientation of a clause depends to a great extent on the verb.

Some verbs convey negative ("odeio" – "hate") or positive ("adooooro" – "loooove"; "prefiro" – "prefer") evaluation by their basic meaning, as in examples (19) and (20).

(19) Pão com ovo. *Adooooro.*

Bread with fried egg. I *loooove* it.

(20) Eu não uso isso. Eu *odeio*. *Prefiro* meus tênis.

I don't wear this. I *hate* it. I *prefer* my tennis shoes.

On the other hand, evaluation conveyed by other verbs can only be identified by the analysis of their arguments. In example (21) and (22) verb "merecer" ("to deserve") can point to a negative or to a positive evaluation, depending on the semantic orientation of its second argument (A2). In (21) semantic orientation is positive ("compliments"), while in (22) it is negative ("jail").

(21) Acompanho e continuarei acompanhando seu trabalho, que merece, sim, *elogios* em muitos pontos.

I follow and I will keep on following your work, which deserves, yes, *compliments* in many aspects.

(22) Ela merece *cadeia*.

She deserves *jail*.

However, there are constructions in which objects cannot be considered arguments of the verb. Neves (2002), following Ashby and Bentivoglio (1993), calls them "constructions with support verbs". In such constructions, the object NP forms a predicate with the verb and thus the construction must be analyzed as a whole. In Brazilian Portuguese, the most productive verbs in such constructions are "dar" ("to give") and "fazer" ("to do", "to make"). In example (23), constructions with support verb "dar" have opposite polarities, and the semantic orientations of the comment must be determined by discourse structure (Taboada, 2016). Conjunction "e" ("and") is usually associated with the idea of additive parataxis. However, it has other uses in Brazilian Portuguese, such as signaling contrast (Camacho, 1999), which is the case in example (23).

> (23) Tinha tudo pra *dar errado* e *deu certo*.
>
> It had everything to *go wrong* and it *went right*.

Neves (2002) presents some reasons why speakers use support verbs, such as the obtainment of more communicative adequacy, more semantic precision and more syntactic versatility. In example (24), the construction with support verb provides more syntactic versatility by the determination of reflexive possession.

> (24) Os pais nunca se dão conta disso não, eles acham q o professor não *faz mais do que a obrigação **deles***... e se quiser ganhar mais trabalhe mais
>
> Parents do not realize this, they think that teachers don't *do more than **their** obligation*... and if teachers want to earn more, they have to work more.

4.2 Constructions and idioms

The construction presented in example (25) is used to convey positive evaluation. The noun "tatuadores" ("tattoo artists") can be replaced by a variety of nouns which nominate, among other possibilities: *i)* professions such as "teachers", "policemen", "doctors" etc; *ii)* human referents such as "mothers", "students", "children" etc; *iii)* animate referents, such as "dogs", "cats", "dolphins" etc; *iv)* inanimate referents, such as "cars", "softwares", "cell phones" etc; *v)* places such as "schools", "churches", "malls" etc.

> (25) *Por mais* tatuadores *como esse…*
>
> *For more* tattoo artists *like this…*

In example (26), the construction conveys negative evaluation. In the first six clauses, the writer of the comment criticizes characteristics and actions of a politician. In the seventh clause, he / she presents the action which he / she considers to be the worst of all. In terms of argumentation, this construction saves the strongest argument for last and can be represented as *Não basta PREDICATION, tem que PREDICATION*.

> (26) Não basta ser golpista, não basta ser corrupto, não basta comprar a grande maioria dos parlamentares, não basta criar 14 mil cargos desnecessários, não basta conceder aumento desproporcional ao STF, não basta extinguir os ministérios da cultura e da previdência social: ele tem que aniquilar os direitos sociais e trabalhistas!
>
> It's not enough to be a state stroker, it's not enough to be corrupt, it's not enough to buy the majority of the parliamentarians, it's not enough to create 14 thousand unnecessary public job roles, it's not enough to grant a disproportionate pay rise to STF, it's not enough to wipe out the ministries of culture and social care: he has to annihilate the social and labor rights!

In idioms, words do not have independent meanings and the idiosyncrasy (meaning cannot be predicted from form) must be stored in the speakers' long-term memory (Jackendoff, 2013). In example (27), idiom "chutar cachorro morto" (literal translation: "to kick a dead dog") in Brazilian Portuguese means being aggressive or even doing harm to somebody who is not able to defend him / herself and is insignificant to society. The idiom is used by the writer of the comment to convey a view of society towards teachers which is growing common: teachers are not important.

> (27) Mexer com professor é como *chutar cachorro morto*, ninguém liga mais.
>
> Messing with teachers is like *kicking a dead dog*, nobody cares.

In example (28), idiom "beijinho no ombro", literally translated as "little kiss over the shoulder" has become one of the most widely used idioms in Brazil after it was used as the chorus and the title of a song by a popular Brazilian funk singer. A quick search on Google, for instance, leads to more than two million results. As it happens with idiom "chutar cachorro morto", its meaning cannot be predicted from the form, as it expresses a gesture of superiority over envious people, negative people who only criticize, haters etc. In the context of the example, the writer of the comment uses the idiom "beijinho no ombro" in order to show that he / she does not care about peoples' critics towards the Facebook page she follows. She sends to those people a "beijinho no ombro" to show that she is superior to their negative and critical behaviour.

> (28) Não curto página de escola, a única com a qual me identifiquei foi essa por justamente mostrar meus medos, anseios enquanto professora. Se não estão satisfeitas, só lamento. *Beijinho no ombro.*
>
> I don't follow pages of schools, the only one I identified myself with was this one exactly because it shows my fears, my yearnings as a teacher. If they are not happy with it, I'm sorry. *Little kiss over the shoulder.*

5   Conclusion and future work

This paper aimed at discussing some challenges found for the creation of a sentiment analysis dictionary for Facebook comments in Brazilian Portuguese.

The analysis of the *corpus* showed that the same words spoken by different people may have polar opposite semantic orientations. We also noticed that the writers of the comments use nouns and noun phrases not only to name some entity, but also to build discourse objects in a way that the label they give to the discourse objects reveals an evaluation. We propound reflections about such problems within the Discourse Analysis framework, mainly Pêcheux (1975) and Mondada and Dubois (1995).

Besides taking into account reflections from Discourse Analysis, another suggestion of the paper is to use assumptions from Construction Grammar to analyze constructions and idioms rather than only nouns, adjectives, NPs, verbs etc. The investigation of constructions and idioms can provide a better understanding of sentiment in text.

In future works, we intend to expand the dictionary and create a test *corpus* in order to try to create algorithms for automatic evaluation of sentiment of Facebook comments in Brazilian Portuguese.

References

W. J. Ashby and P. Bentivoglio. 1993. Information flow in spoken French and Spanish: a comparative study.

Stefano Baccianella, Andrea Esuli, and Fabrizio Sebastiani. 2010. SentiWordNet 3.0: An Enhanced Lexical Resource for Sentiment Analysis and Opinion Mining. *Proceedings of the Seventh International Conference on Language Resources and Evaluation (LREC'10)*, 0(January):2200–2204.

Roberto Gomes Camacho. 1999. Estruturas coordenadas. In Maria Helena Moura Neves, editor, *Gramática do português falado - volume 7*, pages 351–405. Humanitas/FFLCH/USP, S. Paulo.

Lynn Carlson and Daniel Marcu. 2001. Discourse Tagging Reference Manual. Technical report, University of Southern California, Los Angeles.

Facebook. *Company Info*. Available at <www.facebook.com>. Accessed in <07/04/2017>.

Adele E. Goldberg. 2013. Constructionist Approaches. In Elizabeth Closs Traugott and Graeme Trousdale, editors, *The Oxford Handbook of Construction Grammar*, pages 15–31. Oxford University Press, Oxford.

Michael Alexander Kirkwood Halliday. 1985. *An introduction to functional Grammar*. Edward Arnold, Baltimore.

Thomas Hoffmann and Graeme Trousdale. 2013. *The Oxford Handbook of Construction Grammar*. Oxford University Press, Oxford.

Rodolfo Ilari and Renato M. Basso. 2008. O verbo. In Rodolfo Ilari and Maria Helena Moura Neves, editors, *Gramática do português culto falado no brasil - volume 2*, pages 163–365. Ed. da Unicamp, Campinas.

Mikel Iruskieta, Arantza Diaz de Ilarraza, and Mikel Lersundi. 2013. Establishing criteria for RST-based discourse segmentation and annotation for texts in Basque. *Corpus Linguistics and Linguistic Theory*:1–32.

Ray Jackendoff. 2013. Constructions in the parallel architecture. In Thomas Hoffmann and Graeme Trousdale, editors, *The Oxford Handbook of Construction Grammar*, pages 70–92. Oxford University Press, Oxford.

Ingedore G. V. Koch. 2002. *Desvendando os segredos do texto*. Cortez Editora, S. Paulo.

Ingedore G. V. Koch. 2007. *O texto e a construção dos sentidos*. Contexto, S. Paulo.

John Lyons. 1977. *Semantics.*volume 2. Cambridge University Press, Cambridge.

Saif Mohammad, Cody Dunne, and Bonnie Dorr. 2009. Generating high-coverage semantic orientation lexicons from overtly marked words and a thesaurus. *EMNLP '09 Proceedings of the 2009 Conference on Empirical Methods in Natural Language Processing*, 2(August):599–608.

Lorenza Mondada and Danièle Dubois. 1995. Construction des objets de discours et cátegorisation: una approche des processus de référenciation. *Tranel*, 23:273–302.

Maria Helena Moura Neves. 2000. *Gramática de Usos do Português*. Ed. da Unesp, São Paulo.

Maria Helena Moura Neves. 2002. Estudo das construções com verbo-suporte em português. In Ingedore G. V. Koch, editor, *Gramática do português falado - volume 6*, pages 209–238. Editora da Unicamp, Campinas, 2. ed. edition.

Michel Pêcheux. 1975. *Les vérités de la Palice*. Maspero, Paris.

Renata Lopes Rosa. 2015. *Análise de sentimentos e afetividade extraídos das redes sociais*. Ph.D. thesis, USP.

Gwendolyn Seidman. 2014. Expressing the "true Self" on Facebook. *Computers in Human Behavior*, 31(1):367–372.

Maite Taboada. 2016. Sentiment Analysis: An Overview from Linguistics. *Annual Review of Linguistics*, 2(1):325–347.

Maite Taboada, Julian Brooke, Milan Tofiloski, Kimberly Voll, and Manfred Stede. 2011. Lexicon-Based Methods for Sentiment Analysis. *Computational Linguistics*, 37(2):267–307.

Elizabeth Closs Traugott and Graeme Trousdale. 2013. *Constructionalization and constructional changes*. Oxford University Press, Oxford.

R. E. Wilson, S. D. Gosling, and L. T. Graham. 2012. A Review of Facebook Research in the Social Sciences. *Perspectives on Psychological Science*, 7(3):203–220.

Theresa A. Wilson, Janyce Wiebe, and Paul Hoffmann. 2009. Recognizing Contextual Polarity: an exploration of features for phrase-level sentiment analysis. *Computational Linguistics*, 35(3):399–433.

Discourse Segmentation for Building a RST Chinese Treebank

Shuyuan Cao

Universitat Pompeu Fabra (UPF)

shuyuan.cao@hotmail.com

Nianwen Xue

Brandeis University

xuen@brandeis.edu

Iria da Cunha

Universidad Nacional de
Educación a Distancia (UNED)

iriad@flog.uned.es

Mikel Iruskieta
University of Basque Country
(UPV/EHU)

mikel.iruskieta@ehu.eus

Chuan Wang

Brandeis University

cwang24@brandeis.edu

Abstract

Corpus-based discourse analysis of Chinese, as the most spoken language in the world, could be useful for language learning and translation studies. We present here the development of the first free open access Chinese discourse segmented corpus following RST, which can help in the evaluation of automatic segmentation systems and in the development of rhetorical parsers, among other tasks. Our research includes six stages. First, we compile different texts to include in the corpus. Second, we establish discourse segmentation criteria for Chinese. Third, two annotators segment the texts following these rules. Fourth, we calculate the segmentation agreement with Kappa and we analyze the disagreements, including the annotation errors. Fifth, we improve our segmentation criteria. Finally, we elaborate the gold standard discourse segmentation for Chinese, which can be consulted online.

1 Introduction

The emphasis on the idea that discourse information may be useful for Natural Language Processing (NLP) has been increasingly discussed. Discourse information and discourse-based studies are crucial for many NLP tasks (Zhou et al., 2014), such as machine translation (MT) and language learning.

Segmentation is a crucial step of discourse analysis, since it can affect the result of the relational discourse structure. Moreover, discourse segmentation can be useful for different NLP tasks, for instance, the evaluation of automatic segmentation systems, and the development of discourse parsers and automatic summarizers.

Corpus-based research is another important aspect for NLP tasks. As Wu (2014) indicates, corpora offer a large amount of language information in a quick and effective way. Corpus-based approach has been applied to different NLP tasks, such as information retrieval, parsing and machine translation (MT), among others.

Chinese is the world's most spoken language and occupies an important position in the NLP research field. However, corpus-based studies with discourse information for Chinese are still few, especially for Chinese discourse segmentation. This paper aims to present the first accessible segmented Chinese corpus according to RST and enriched with part-of-speech (POS) information.

In the second section, we introduce the theoretical framework of this study. In the third section, we discuss some related works. In the fourth section, we present the detailed information of our corpus. In the fifth section, we explain the methodology for elaborating the segmentation criteria In the sixth section, we show results and limitations of this work. In the seventh section, we show our final segmentation criteria and present an error analysis. Finally, conclusions and future work are outlined in the last section.

Proceedings of the 6th Workshop Recent Advances in RST and Related Formalisms, pages 73–81,
Santiago de Compostela, Spain, September 4 2017. ©2017 Association for Computational Linguistics

2   Theoretical Framework

Rhetorical Structure Theory (RST) (Mann and Thompson, 1988) is a theory that was created especially for discourse analysis and it has been selected as the theoretical framework of this work. It focuses on the hierarchical structure of a whole text, where discourse relations can be annotated within a sentence (intra-sentence style) and between sentences (inter-sentence style). Intra-sentence and inter-sentence annotation styles help to inform how discourse elements are being expressed in a language, and translation strategies (if any) can be detected in different levels of an RS-tree (da Cunha and Iruskieta, 2010; Iruskieta, da Cunha and Taboada, 2015).

RST addresses both hierarchical and relational aspects of text structures for discourse analysis. Elementary Discourse Units (EDUs) (Marcu, 2000) and coherence relations are established in RST. Relations are recursive in RST and are hold between EDUs, which can be Nuclei or Satellites. Satellites offer additional information about nuclei. EDUs can be linked among them holding a nucleus-satellite (e.g. CAUSE, JUSTIFY, EVIDENCE, CONCESSION) function or a multinuclear (e.g. CONJUNCTION, LIST, SEQUENCE) function. As relations are recursive, all the discourse units of the text have a function in a treelike structure, if and only if the text is coherent.

3   State of the art

3.1   RST Based Discourse Segmentation

On the one hand, several corpora for different languages have been annotated under RST. Authors of these corpora have established their own segmentation criteria for different discourse analysis tasks. Some of these corpora are: (i) for English, the RST Discourse Treebank (Carlson, Marcu and Okurowski, 2001)[1] and the Discourse Relations Reference Corpus (Taboada and Renkema, 2008)[2]; (ii) for German, the Potsdam Commentary Corpus (Stede and Neumann, 2014)[3]; (iii) for Spanish, the RST Spanish Treebank (da Cunha, Torres-Moreno and Sierra, 2011; da Cunha et al., 2011)[4]; (iv) for Basque, the RST Basque Treebank (Iruskieta et al., 2013[5]; (v) for Portuguese, the CorpusTCC (Pardo, Nunes and Rino, 2008) and *Rhetalho* (Pardo and Seno, 2005)[6]; (vi) for Spanish, Basque and English, the Multilingual RST Treebank (Iruskieta, da Cunha and Taboada, 2015)[7].

On the other hand, some available discourse segmentation systems based on RST exist. For example: i) for English (Tofiloski, Brooke and Taboada, 2009)[8], ii) for Spanish (da Cunha et al., 2012)[9], and iii) for Basque (Iruskieta and Zapirain, 2015)[10].

3.2   Discourse Segmentation for Chinese

Few works focus on the Chinese segmentation from the discourse level. The Penn Chinese Treebank (Xue, 2005) is especially designed for Chinese discourse analysis with the Penn Discourse TreeBank (PDTB) (Miltsakaki et al. 2004) style. In this work, segmentation criteria are based on connectives and different types of conjunctions. Under RST, there are three works that use form-based criteria that based on punctuation marks to elaborate segmentation rules for Chinese (Yue, 2006; Qiu, 2010; Li, Feng and Zhou 2013).

There are other two notable works related to Chinese discourse segmentation (Xue and Yang, 2011; Yang and Xue, 2012; Xu and Li, 2013), which focus on the influence of the comma for Chinese segmentation.

---

[1] `https://catalog.ldc.upenn.edu/LDC2002T07` [Last consulted: 06 of July of 2017]

[2] `http://www.sfu.ca/rst/06tools/discourse_relati ons_corpus.html` [Last consulted: 06 of July of 2017]

[3] `http://angcl.ling.uni-potsdam.de/resources/pcc.html` [Last consulted: 06 of July of 2017]

[4] `http://corpus.iingen.unam.mx/rst/citar.html` [Last consulted: 06 of July of 2017]

[5] `http://ixa2.si.ehu.es/diskurtsoa/en/` [Last consulted: 06 of July of 2016]

[6] `http://www.icmc.usp.br/~taspardo/projects.htm` [Last consulted: 06 of July of 2017]

[7] `http://ixa2.si.ehu.es/rst/` [Last consulted: 06 of July of 2017]

[8] `https://www.sfu.ca/~mtaboada/SLSeg.html` [Last consulted: 06 of July of 2017]

[9] `http://dev.termwatch.es/esj/DiSeg/WebDiSeg/` [Last consulted: 06 of July of 2017]

[10] `http://ixa2.si.ehu.es/EusEduSeg/EusEduSeg.pl` [Last consulted: 06 of July of 2017]

Previous segmentation criteria were based on linguistic form, but our segmentation criteria for Chinese are also based in linguistic function.

4 Research Corpus

Complexity of discourse structure and heterogeneity are the main characteristics taken into account for the corpus development. The specific considerations are the following: (a) texts with different sizes (between 100 and 2,000 words), (b) specialized texts and non-specialized texts, (c) texts from different domains, (d) texts from different genres, (e) texts from different original publications, and (f) texts from different authors.

Based on the mentioned aspects, finally, we have selected 50 Chinese texts to form our research corpus. The genres of the texts are four: (a) abstracts of research papers, (b) news, (c) advertisements, and (d) announcements. The longest text of the corpus contains 1,774 words and the shortest one contains 111 words. Table 1 shows the genre statistics of the corpus.

The sources of these texts are: (a) International Conference about Terminology (1997), (b) Shanghai Miguel Cervantes Library, (c) Chamber of Commerce and Investment of China in Spain, (d) Spain Embassy in Beijing, (e) Spain-China Council Foundation, (f) Confucius Institute Foundation in Barcelona, (g) Beijing Cervantes Institute and (h) Granada Confucius Institute.

The corpus includes texts related to seven domains: (a) terminology (15 texts), (b) culture (6 texts), (c) language (8 texts), (d) economy (7 texts), (e) education (4 texts), (f) art (5 texts), and (g) international affairs (5 texts).

The corpus was enriched automatically with POS information by using the Stanford parser (Levy and Manning, 2003) for Chinese.

Finally, we have created an online interface to access the research corpus: http://ixa2.si.ehu.es/rst/zh/. Users can search POS information[11] and discourse segments of each text in the research corpus. Moreover, users can also download the texts of the corpus.

---

[11] For more detailed information about the POS information about the corpus, consult Cao, da Cunha and Iruskieta (2016) and Cao, da Cunha and Iruskieta (2017).

Genre	Texts	Original publication
Abstract of research paper	15	International Conference about Terminology (1997)
News	15	Shanghai Miguel Cervantes Library, Chamber of Commerce and Investment of China in Spain, Spain Embassy in Beijing, Confucius Institute Foundation in Barcelona
Advertisement	13	Shanghai Miguel Cervantes Library, Spain-China Council Foundation, Beijing Cervantes Institute, Granada Confucius Institute
Announcement	7	Spain Embassy in Beijing, Confucius Institute Foundation in Barcelona, Beijing Cervantes Institute
Total	50	

Table 1: Corpus source information

5 Methodology

First of all, we elaborate a preliminary discourse segmentation criteria proposal for Chinese based on linguistic function (the function of the syntactic components) and linguistic form (punctuation category and verbs). We have not considered the meaning (of any coherence relation between propositions) to segment EDUs to avoid circularity in the annotation process. For the function and form perspective, we adopt the segmentation criteria from Iruskieta, da Cunha and Taboada (2015).

The following segmentation criteria are used in out work:

* Paragraphs and line breaks. In our study, a line break will be taken as an independent EDU to segment the titles (and subtitles).

(Ex.1) Text name: FCEC1

Text: [亲爱的朋友们，] [...]

English: [Dear friends,] [...]

Explanation: The Chinese passage starts with a greeting, it is followed by a comma and there is a line break.

- Sentences and periods. In our study, the period marks the end of an independent EDU.

(Ex.2) Text name: ICP4

Text: [塞万提斯学院正式教师职位招聘在西班牙媒体上公布。] [同时也在塞万提斯学院网站发布信息。]

English: [Cervantes Institute official professor recruitment notice publishes on Spanish media.] [Meanwhile, also publishes on the Cervantes Institute webpage.]

Explanation: After the word "*gongbu*" (公布) ('publish'), there is a period, followed by another sentence.

- Question mark and exclamation mark. Both marks are signals of a sentence boundary.

(Ex.3) Text name: TERM34

Text: [区分界限在哪里？] [区分表语及非表语的关键在哪里？] [涉及文字关系、背景联系、物主关系还是其它方面？]

English: [Distinguish boundary in where?] [Distinguish predicative and non-predicative of key in where?] [About characters relation, background relation, possessive relation or other aspect?]

Explanation: At the end of each sentence, there is a question mark.

- Other EDUs should have a main verb or an adjunct verb phrase.[12] This is a basic segmentation criterion and segmentation criteria bellow should follow this rule.

(Ex.4) Text name: CCICE3

Text: [10 月份，西班牙财政部共**筹集** 143.99 亿欧元，共拍卖国债四次。]

English: [The month of October the Treasury **raised** 14.399 millions in four issues.][13]

Explanation: The Chinese word "*chouji*" (筹集) is a verb and means 'raise' in English.

- Discourse Marker (DM)[14], verb and comma. If there is a DM at the beginning of a sentence and, this sentence is divided into two parts by a comma (each one including a verb), both parts are considered independent EDUs.

(Ex.5) Text name: TERM31

Text: [由于经常使用词法句型模式，] [用以分析文本或者至少说明性略语较为合适。]

English: [**Due to** often uses morph-syntax models,] [to analyze texts or at least illustrative abbreviations.]

Explanation: The Chinese DM "*youyu*" (由于) ('due to') is placed at the beginning of the first EDU, and a comma is included in the sentence. Besides, the first EDU includes the Chinese verb "*shiyong*" (使用) ('use'), while the second EDU includes the verb "*fenxi*" (分析) ('analyze').

(Ex.6) Text name: TERM19

Text: [此时，标准不但会失效，] [而且也不能发挥作用。]

English: [In this condition, standardization not only ceases to be effective,] [**but also** could not play its role.]

Explanation: The Chinese DM "*er*" (而且) ('but also') appears after a comma in the sentence. In addition, verbs are included in both EDUs: "*shixiao*" (失效) ('lose effectiveness') in the first EDU, and "*fahui*" (发挥) ('exert') in the second EDU.

- Semicolon plus adjunct verb phrase.

(Ex.7) Text name: TERM34

Text: [例如，形容词 marginal（边上的）在英语中可用于参照语和谓语，例如"边缘注释 (marginal not)" 以及"边缘个案 (marginal case)"；] [相反，在"名词非表语性形容词"一类中，尽管采用了形容词的定义，但是与名词发挥的作用类似，比如：linguistic difficulties（语言上的困难）/language difficulties（语言困难）。]

English: [For example, adjective marginal (something besides) in English can be used referential and predicate, for example, "marginal note" and "marginal case";] [in contrast, in "noun but not predicative adjective" category, although adapts adjective definition, with noun works function similar, such as, linguistic difficulties/language difficulties]

---

[12] In RST clauses (adverbial clauses) are considered EDUs, except for complement clauses (Mann and Thompson, 1988).

[13] Here we give an English literal translation for each example in order to let the readers understand.

[14] In this work, the definition of DM that we follow is based on Portolés (2001). DMs are invariable linguistic units that depend on the following aspects: (a) distinct morph-syntactic properties, (b) semantics and pragmatics and (c) inferences that are made in the communication.

Explanation: A semicolon separates the text into two parts, and each EDU includes a Chinese verb: the verb "*yong*" (用) ('apply to') in the first EDU and the verb "*shiyong*" (使用) ('use') in the second EDU.

- Parenthetical and dash. Only when a parenthetical unit does not modify a noun neither an adjective and it includes a verb, it is an independent segment; if within the parenthetical unit there are coordinated parts, the coordinated parts are also segmented[15].

(Ex.8) Text name: TERM18

Text: [确实，术语数据库的设计和管理无论在理论和方法论] [(如何表示一个术语？] [有最简单的表达方法吗？] [术语之间如何分类？)] [⋯]

English: [Indeed, the design and management of the terminology database no matter in theory and methodology,] [(how to express a terminology?] [is there the easiest way to express?] [how to distinguish among terminologies?]) [...]

Explanation: The parenthetical unit does not modify its previous part; it should be an independent segment. The sentences "*ruhe biaoshi yige shuyu*?" (如何表示一个术语？) (How to express a term?), "*you zuijiandan de fangfa ma*?" (有最简单的方法吗？) (Is there the easiest way to express?) and "*shuyu zhijian ruhe fenlei*?" (术语之间如何分类？) (How to distinguish among terminologies?) include a verb and are coordinated parts in this parenthetical unit with verbs and question marks

- Coordination and ellipsis with verbs. Coordinated clauses with verbs are considered independent EDUs (even they include a null subject).

(Ex.9) Text name: TERM25

Text: [...] [自 1994 年以来**我们**在德武斯特大学进行法律领域专业文件的翻译工作，] [**我们**希望能按照实际情况呈现出这些年工作中碰到的问题以及取得的成就。] [...]

---

[15] This criterion only exists in our work; the mentioned Chinese segmentation works have overlooked this segmentation criterion.

English: [From 1994 until now we in Deusto University **carry out** law campus professional document of translation works,] [we **hope** can follow real situation present these years works encounter problems and achievement] [...]

Explanation: In the Chinese text, the two coordinated clauses include verbs ("*jinxing*" [进行] ['to carry out'] and "*xiwang*" [希望] ['hope']).

- Relative, modifying and appositive clauses. Relative clauses, clauses that modifies a noun or adjective or appositive clauses are not considered independent EDUs.

(Ex.10) Text name: BMCS5

Text: [现代化的交流工具（**聊天，论坛，博客，wiki 和电子邮件**），辅助学生在任何地方都与组内同伴交流互动。]

English: [Modern communications tools (chats, forums, blogs, wiki and emails), helps students in anywhere with inside group companions interact.]

Explanation: The names of the communication tools in the parenthetical part are appositives of the "*xiandaihua de jiaoliugongju*" (现代化的交流工具) ('modern communication tools').

- Reported speech. In this study, we do not consider reported speech as an independent EDU.

- Truncated EDUs. For the cases of truncated EDUs, we use the non-relation label of Sameunit (Carlson, Marcu and Okurowski, 2003).

6 Result

In this work, we use Cohen Kappa to measure inter-annotator agreement between the two corpus annotators (A1 and A2). Previous works use Kappa to measure the agreement between two annotators in RST discourse segmentation (Iruskieta, Diaz de Ilarraza and Lersundi 2015). Kappa calculates the agreement between annotators as:

$$K = \frac{P(A) - P(E)}{1 - P(E)}$$

where (A) represents the current observed agreement, and P(E) represents chance agreement. Kappa was calculated by considering titles, parentheses, and verbs, as EDUs candidates. Table 2 includes the statistics used to measure the agreement between both annotators.

Other discourse evaluation measures have been employed to address the problematic of discourse evaluation measures. See Fournier (2013), and Sidarenka, Peldszus and Stede (2015) for further details.

Annotator		A2		Total
		Yes	No	
A1	Yes	765	101	866
	No	204	1888	2092
Total		969	1989	2958

Table 2: Segmentation cross tabulation

Table 3 includes the Kappa agreement results regarding each part of the corpus. The highest agreement between both annotators is 0.815, and the lowest agreement is 0.616. The agreement for the whole corpus is 0.76, which means the preliminary segmentation criteria are reliable for Chinese.

Corpus Source	Kappa Agreement
ICT	0.815
SMCL	0.719
CCICS	0.744
SEB	0.711
SCCF	0.711
CIFB	0.616
BCI	0.759
GCI	0.705
Total	0.76

Table 3: K results regarding each part of the corpus

7 Analysis of Corpus Annotation

After obtaining the evaluation of segmentation results, we analyze the disagreement sources between both annotators to establish the gold standard segmentation for our corpus. The following cases summarize the segmentation errors and include an example of the final segmentation decision:

- **Title**

A1: [2.] [术语构建] (×)

[2.] [Terminology construction]

A2: [2. 术语构建] (√)[16]

[2. Terminology construction]

Analysis: A1 has divided the title into two parts due to the period. However, we do not segment any element in a title or subtitle.

- **Comma + DM + verb**

A1: [这些内容不仅丰富了术语内容，] [同时还引起了一些术语基本定义的争论。] (√)

[These things have enriched the content of terms,] [**meanwhile** also cause some debates of the basic definition of terminology.]

A2: [这些内容不仅丰富了术语内容，同时还引起了一些术语基本定义的争论。] (×)

[These things have enriched the content of terms, meanwhile also cause some debates of the basic definition of terminology.]

Analysis: A1 has divided the sentence into two parts due to the comma. This segmentation is correct, because the discourse marker "*tongshi*" (同时) ('meanwhile') appears after the coma. Besides, the two parts have the same subject, and there is a verb "*fengfu*" (丰富) ('enrich') in the first EDU and another verb "*yinqi*" (引起) ('cause') in the second EDU.

- **Colon**

A1: [各种语言中唯一一致的命名参照物的情况是：] [术语均从英语中来。] (√)

[For all languages the only consistent reference is:] [all terminologies **come** from English.]

A2: [各种语言中唯一一致的命名参照物的情况是：术语均从英语中来。] (×)

[For all languages the only consistent reference is: all terminologies **come** from English.]

Analysis: A1 has divided the sentence into two parts due to the colon. In the preliminary version of segmentation criteria, colon was not considered; therefore, there is a disagreement regarding this punctuation mark between both annotators. We decide to segment the part after colon, because both EDUs include verbs: "*mingming*" (命名) ('to give name') in the first EDU and "*lai*" (来) ('come') in the second EDU.

---

[16] In this work, we use "√" to represent the correct segmentation and "×" to represent the incorrect segmentation. A1 represents the first annotator and A2 means the second annotator.

- **Temporal adverb clause + comma + verb clause**

A1: ［当上述内容均能在同一片文章中准确描述后，］[我们便能做到建立巴斯克语的 "法律论述体系"。] (√)

[**When** all the previous mentioned can be **described** in the same passage,] [we can **establish** the "legal discourse system" for Basque.]

A2: [当上述内容均能在同一片文章中准确描述后，我们便能做到建立巴斯克语的 "法律论述体系"。] (×)

[**When** all the previous mentioned can be **described** in the same passage, we can **establish** the "legal discourse system" for Basque.]

Analysis: A1 has divided the sentence into two parts due to the comma. The temporal adverb "*dang*" (当) ('when') and the comma can be considered as a segmentation boundary, because both EDUs include a verb: "*miaoshu*" (描述) ('describe') in the first EDU and "*jianli*" (建立) ('establish') in the second EDU.

- **Wrong EDU without verbs**

A1: [包括 12 副绘画作品和 2 副达利的原创作品，] [以及 205 份杂志、报纸及宣传单。] (×)

[**Including** 12 paintings and 2 original works of Dalí,] [and 205 magazines, newspapers and advertisements.]

A2: [包括 12 副绘画作品和 2 副达利的原创作品，以及 205 份杂志、报纸及宣传单。] (√)

[**Including** 12 paintings and 2 original works of Dalí, and 205 magazines, newspapers and advertisements.]

Analysis: A1 has divided the sentence into two parts because it is a coordinated sentence. However, the segmentation of the annotator A1 is not correct because there is no verb in the second EDU. The only verb in this sentence is "*baokuo*" (包括) ('include').

Based on the error analysis, we have improved our segmentation criteria. Meanwhile, we give a debate between discourse experts and, taking our segmentation criteria into account, we have chosen the best segmentation option in case of disagreement.

Hence, we have created the gold standard segmented corpus for Chinese. This gold standard will be the basis for the discourse annotation of the corpus.

Table 4 shows the final criteria used for the discourse segmentation. We have divided the segmentation criteria into two types: EDU criteria and Non-EDU criteria.

Criteria to form an EDU	Non EDU criteria
Every EDU should have an adjunct verb clause	Relative, modifying and appositive clauses
Paragraphs with line breaks (titles)	Reported speech
Period and question exclamation marks	Truncated EDUs (same-unit)
Comma + adjunct verb clause	
Semicolon + adjunct verb clause	
Colon + adjunct verb clause	
Parenthetical & dash + adjunct verb clause	
Coordination with two adjunct verb clauses	

Table 4: Final discourse segmentation criteria

8 Conclusion and Future Work

In this work, we have presented the RST discourse segmentation criteria used to annotate a Chinese corpus including texts from different domains, textual genres, sources, authors and length. Two annotators have annotated the corpus and inter-annotator agreement has been measured with Kappa, obtaining adequate results. Moreover, we carry out an error analysis to obtain the final gold standard discourse segmented corpus for Chinese following RST. This corpus can be downloaded and consulted online. Users can use the search tool to find information in the corpus related to discourse segments and POS categories in Chinese.

In the future, we will carry out the annotation of the coherence RST relations of these texts, which is one of the most difficult challenges for annotation works (Hovy and Lavid, 2010).

References

Cao Shuyuan, da Cunha Iria, and Iruskieta Mikel. 2016. A Corpus-based Approach for Spanish-Chinese Language Learning. In *Proceedings of the 3rd Workshop on Natural Language Processing Techniques for Educational Applications (NLP-TEA3)*, 97-106.

Cao Shuyuan, da Cunha Iria, and Iruskieta Mikel. 2017. Toward the Elaboration of a Spanish-Chinese Parallel Annotated Corpus. *EPiC Series in Language and Linguistics*, 2: 315-324.

Carlson Lynn, Marcu Daniel, and Okurowski Mary Ellen. 2001. Building a Discourse-Tagged Corpus in the Framework of Rhetorical Structure Theory. In *Proceedings of the 2nd SIGDIAL Workshop on Discourse Dialogue*, 1-10.

da Cunha Iria and Iruskieta Mikel. 2010. Comparing rhetorical structures of different languages: The influence of translation strategies. *Discourse Studies*, 12(5): 563-598.

da Cunha Iria; SanJuan, Eric; Torres-Moreno, Juan-Manuel; Lloberes, Marina; and Castellón, Irene. 2012. DiSeg 1.0: The First System for Spanish Discourse Segmentation. *Expert Systems with Applications (ESWA)*, 39(2): 1671-1678.

da Cunha Iria, Torres-Moreno Juan-Manuel, and Sierra, Gerardo. 2011. On the Development of the RST Spanish Treebank. In *Proceedings of the 5th Linguistic Annotation Workshop at ACL'2011*, 1-10.

da Cunha Iria; Torres-Moreno Juan-Manuel; Sierra Gerardo; Cabrera-Diego Luis Adrián; Castro Rolón Brenda Gabriela; and Rolland Bartilotti Juan Miguel. 2011. The RST Spanish Treebank On-line Interface. In *Proceedings of Recent Advances in Natural Language Processing (RANLP' 2011)*, 698-703.

Fournier Chris. 2013. Evaluating Text Segmentation using Boundary Edit Distance. In *Proceedings of the 51st Annual Meeting of the Association for Computational Linguistics (ACL' 2013)*, 1702-1712.

Hovy Eduard, and Lavid Julia. 2010. Toward a 'Science' of Corpus Annotation: A New Methodology Challenges for Corpus Linguistics. *International Journal of Translation*, 22(1): 13-36.

Iruskieta Mikel, Aranzabe María Jesús, Diaz de Ilarraza Arantza, Gonzalez-Dios Itziar, Lersundi, Mikel and Lopez de Lacalle Oier. 2013. The RST Basque TreeBank: an online search interface to check rhetorical relations. In *Proceedings of IV Workshop A RST e os Estudos do Texto*, 40-49.

Iruskieta Mikel, da Cunha Iria, and Taboada Maite. 2015. A Qualitative Comparison Method for Rhetorical Structures: Identifying different discourse structures in multilingual corpora. *Language resources and evaluation*, 49(2): 263-309.

Iruskieta Mikel, Diaz de Ilarraza Arantza, and Lersundi Mikel. 2015. Establishing criteria for RST-based discourse segmentation and annotation for texts in Basque. *Corpus Linguistics and Linguistic Theory*, 11(2): 303-334.

Iruskieta Mikel and Zapirain Benat. 2015. EusEduSeg: A Dependency-Based EDU Segmentation for Basque. *Procesamiento del Lenguaje Natural*, 55: 41-48.

Levy Roger and Manning Christopher. 2003. Is it harder to parse Chinese, or the Chinese Treebank? In *Proceedings of the 41st Annual Meeting of the Association for Computational Linguistics (ACL' 2003)*, 439-446.

Li Yancui, Feng Wenhe, and Zhou Guodong. 2012. Elementary Discourse Unit in Chinese Dsicourse Structure Analysis. *Chinese Lexical Semantics*, 7717: 186-198.

Mann William C. and Thompson Sandra A. 1988. Rhetorical Structure Theory: Toward a functional theory of text organization. *Text&Talk*, 8(3): 243-281.

Marcu Daniel. 2000. The rhetorical parsing of unrestricted texts: A surface-based approach. *Computational Linguistics*, 26(3): 395-448.

Miltsakaki Eleni, Prasad Rashmi, Joshi Aravind, and Webber Bonnie. 2004. The Penn Discourse Treebank. In *Proceedings of 4th International Conference on Language Resources and Evaluation* (*LREC' 2004*), 2237-2240.

Mayor Aingeru, Alegría Iñaki, Díaz de Llarrarza Sánchez, Labaka Goka, Lersundi Mikel, and Sarasola Kepa. 2009. Evaluación de un sistema de traducción automática basado en reglas o por qué BLEU sólo sirve para lo que sirve. *Procesamiento del Lenguaje Natural*, 43: 197-205.

Pardo Thiago A. S., Nunes Maria Maria das Graças V., and Rino Lucia H. M. 2008. Dizer: An Automatic Discourse Analyzer for Brazilian Portuguese. *Lecture Notes in Artificial Intelligence*, 3171:224-234.

Pardo Thiago A. S. and Seno Eloize R. M. 2005. Rhetalho: um corpus dereferência anotado retoricamente. *Anais do V Encontro de Corpora*. São Carlos-SP, Brasil.

Pórtoles José. 2001. *Marcadores del discursivo*. 4th edition. Barcelona: Ariel.

Qiu Wusong. 2010. *Jiyu xiucijiegoulilun de hanyuxinwenpinglun yupianjiegou yanjiu* (基于修辞结构理论的汉语新闻评论语篇研究 *[Analysis of Discourse Structure in Chinese News Commentaries under Rhetorical Structure Theory]*). Master thesis. Nanjing: Nanjing Normal University.

Sidarenka Uladzimir, Peldszus Andreas, and Stede Manfred. 2015. Discourse Segmentation of German

Texts. *Journal for Language Technology and Computational Linguistics*, 30(1): 71-98.

Stede Manfred and Neumann Arne. 2014. Potsdam Commentary Corpus 2.0: Annotation for Discourse Research. In *Proceedings of the International Conference on Language Resources and Evaluation (LREC' 2014)*, 925-929.

Taboada Maite and Renkema Jan. 2008. *Discourse Relations Reference Corpus* [Corpus]. Simon Fraser University and Tilburg University.

Tofiloski Milan, Brooke Julian, and Taboada Maite. 2009. A Syntactic and Lexical-Based Discourse Segmenter. In *Proceedings of the 47th Annual Meeting of the Association for Computational Linguistics (ACL' 2009)*, 77–80.

Wilks Yorick. *Machine Translation: Its scope and limits.* New York: Spring.

Wu Shangyi. 2014. On Application of computer-based corpora in translation. In *Proceedings of 2nd International Conference on Computer, Electrical, and Systems Sciences, and Engineering (CESSE' 2014)*, 173-178.

Xu Shengqin, and Li Peifeng. 2013. Recognizing Chinese Elementary Discourse Unit on Comma. In *Proceedings of International Conference on Asian Language Processing (IALP' 2013)*, 3-6.

Xue Nianwen. 2005. Annotating discourse connectives in the Chinese Treebank. In *Proceedings of the Workshop on Frontiers in Corpus Annotation II: Pie in the Sky at ACL' 2005*, 84-91.

Xue Nianwen and Yang Yaqin. 2011. Chinese sentences segmentation as comma classification. In *Proceedings of the 49th Annual Meeting of the Association for Computational Linguistics (ACL 2011)*, 631-635.

Yang Yaqin and Xue Nianwen. 2012. Chinese Comma Disambiguation for Discourse Analysis. In *Proceedings of the 50th Annual Meeting of the Association for Computational Linguistics (ACL' 2012)*, 786-794.

Yue Ming. 2006. *Hanyu caijingpinglun de xiucijiegou biaozhu ji pianzhangyanjiu* (汉语财经评论的修辞结构标注及篇章研究 [Annotation and Analysis of Chinese Financial News Commentaries in terms of Rhetorical Structure]). PhD thesis, Beijing: Communication University of China.

Zhou Lanjun, Li Binyang, Wei Zhongyu, and Wong Kam-Fai. 2014. The CUHK Discourse Treebank for Chinese: Annotating Explicit Discourse Connectives for the Chinese Treebank. In *Proceedings of the International Conference on Language Resources and Evaluation (LREC' 2014)*, 942-949.

Zhou Yuping and Xue Nianwen. 2012. PDTB-style discourse annotation of Chinese text. In *Proceedings of the 50th Annual Meeting of the Association for Computational Linguistics (ACL' 2012)*, 69-77.

Zhou Yuping and Xue Nianwen. 2015. The Chinese Discourse TreeBank: a Chinese corpus annotated with discourse relations. *Language Resources and Evaluation*, 49(2): 397-431.

Authors Index